If Wishes Were Horses

If Wishes Were Horses

Quotations & Proverbs
For Horse People

Deborah Eve Rubin

copyright © 1995 by D. E. Rubin

Library of Congress Cataloging-in-Publication Data

Rubin, Deborah Eve, 1954–
   If wishes were horses : quotations & proverbs for horse
people / Deborah Eve Rubin.
      p. cm.
   Includes bibliographical references and indexes.
   ISBN 0-87842-305-2 : $12.00
   1. Horses—Quotations, maxims, etc. 2. Proverbs. I. Title.
PN6084.H66R93 1994   94-24174
636.1—dc20   CIP

Mountain Press Publishing Company
P.O. Box 2399 • Missoula, MT 59806
406-728-1900 • 800-234-5308

For my ponies,
Princess and Chief

Contents

Introduction

If you go to your local library and look in any standard book of quotations, you'll probably find several entries related to horses. You might even find some not included here. But this is one of the few books devoted exclusively to quotations, proverbs and sayings on matters equine and equestrian.

Why devote such a book entirely to the horse? Few other animals have played so crucial a role in the development of the modern world. As someone once said, "Mankind rode to civilization on the back of a horse." What other animal combines such strength with delicacy, wonderment with the commonplace? Horses have long been a source of inspiration to poets, authors and just plain folks.

From the sublime to the ridiculous, from love to hate, from birth to death and everything in between, it's all here. And not just horses, but their equine relatives, both real—ponies, donkeys, mules—and fantastic—unicorns, winged horses, centaurs.

So if your good horse is a bad color, or your bad horse eats twice as much as your good one, relax. You may not be able to do anything about the situation, but at least you can share what others in the same position have had to say about it.

About This Book

If Wishes Were Horses is divided into four sections—Horses & Ponies; Donkeys & Mules; Horsemanship, Work & Sport; and Unicorns & Others—based on the primary emphasis of the quotations. While some quotations might fit equally well into another section, each appears only once.

Two indexes follow the four sections of quotations: An extensive key word index allows you to locate quotations on many varied aspects of the horse world, while the author index allows you to find someone in particular. All quotations are numbered, and the key words are indexed to the quotation number, not page number. Every effort has been made to provide relevant dates for each author and each quotation, although in some cases that information simply is not available (or couldn't be found).

Abbreviations

anon.	anonymous
b.	born
B.C.E.	before the common era (equivalent to B.C.)
bk.	book
ca.	circa
C.E.	of the common era (equivalent to A.D.)
ch.	chapter
d.	died
fl.	flourished
fo.	folio
no.	number
p.	page
pt.	part
sat.	satire
sc.	scene
sec.	section
st.	stanza
v.	verse
vol.	volume

Part One

Horses & Ponies

1. The horse, the noblest, bravest, proudest, most courageous, and certainly the most perverse and infuriating animal that humans ever domesticated.

Anne McCaffrey (1926–), *The Lady* (1987).

2. A horse is wonderful by definition.

Piers Anthony (1934–), *Virtual Mode* (1991).

3. God first made man. He thought better of it and made woman. When he got the time he made the horse, which had the courage and spirit of man and the beauty and grace of woman.

Brazilian saying

4. I think a horse is a four-legged animal that is produced by two other horses, and if it happens to be a young horse or an old horse, it's still a horse and you can't make it into anything else.

Montgomery County Circuit Court Judge
Richard B. Latham, in Dowd,
"Some Horsing Around Up In Montgomery,"
The Washington Star, October 1, 1977, sec. A.

5. In the beginning man was a wild horse.

Stan Steiner (1925–1985),
Dark and Dashing Horsemen (1981).

6. Horses and dogs have been man's most intimate and faithful companions since the dawn of history, but the horse has certainly been the most useful. In sport, agriculture, transport and warfare, the horse has contributed more to human pleasure, ambition and progress than any other animal.

Prince Philip (1921–), foreword to Monique and
Hans B. Dossenbach, *The Noble Horse* (1987).

7. I hold that no trade founded on horses can be construed as base. Didn't the word "knight" once mean simply "one who rides a horse?"

L. Sprague deCamp (1907–) and
Catherine Crook deCamp (1907–),
The Incorporated Knight (1987).

8. Horses, like babies, are there only to be admired.

Marcia S. Copper, *The Horseman's Etiquette Book* (1976).

9. A horse should be treated like a gentleman.

Leland Stanford (1824–1893)

10. A girl needs a horse. But does a horse need a girl.

> Piers Anthony (1934–), *Virtual Mode* (1991).

11. Horses are born trying to commit suicide.

> anon.

12. Thoroughbreds are born trying to commit suicide.

> anon.

13. Never inspect the teeth of a gift horse.

> St. Jerome (ca. 400), preface to
> *Commentary on the Epistle to the Ephesians* (340–420).

14. Always look a gift horse in the mouth.

> anon.

15. A gift horse looked in the mouth will remove your nose.

> June H. Murphy, 1980s greeting card

16. I am resolved to ride this way [facing the tail], to make good the proverb, that I may not look a gift horse in the mouth.

> Richard Head (1637–1686) and Francis Kirkman
> (1632–1680), *The English Rogue*, pt. 3 (1674).

17. Who the hell am I to look a
gift horse in the mouth?

> G. H. Coxe (1901–?),
> *Murder for Two* (1943).

18. . . . that we must not look a
gift horse in the mouth. . . .
Some people have a knack of putting upon
you gifts of no real value, to engage you to
substantial gratitude.

> Charles Lamb (1775–1834), "Popular Fallacies,"
> *Last Essays of Elia (1826)*.

19. The policy of not looking a gift horse in the
mouth may easily be carried too far.

> William Allingham (1824–1889),
> Rambles in England and Ireland, 2 (1873).

20. Don't look a given horse in the teeth.

> Russian proverb

21. Don't look at the teeth of a horse that you
borrow.

> Philippine proverb

22. When they offer you a horse don't look at its teeth.

Greek proverb

23. I have never looked a gift horse in the mouth: not that I lack curiosity, but none of my husband's patients ever happened to give him a horse.

Marguerite H. Wolf (1914–?),
in Tufts Folia Medica 8:115 (1962).

24. A gift horse may not be looked in the teeth.

John Stanbridge (1463–1510),
Vulgaria (ca. 1520, posthumously).

25. They need not look in your mouth to know your age.

James Kelly (ca. 1720)

26. Never look a gift horse in the mouth. Outside of it being unsanitary, it might bite you.

Day Keene (d. 1969),
Framed in Guilt (1949).

27. Don't stick your nose in the gift horse's oral cavity.

M. P. Hood, Sin (1963).

28. He always looked a gift horse in the mouth.

François Rabelais (1494–1553),
Gargantua, bk. 1, ch. 11 (1534).

29. Do not trouble about the color of a gift horse.

Italian proverb

30. If you meet a piebald horse, wish before you see his tail.

New Forest (England) Gypsy proverb

31. Spring and autumn are riding on a piebald mare.

Russian proverb

32. Such horses as have too much white upon their face, are said to have moist brains, and consequently to be subject to many infirmities.

The Sieur de Solleysell,
*The Compleat Horseman: Discovery of the
Surest Marks of the Beauty, Goodness,
Faults and Imperfections of Horses* (1696).

33. When the mare has a bald face, the filly will have a blaze.

John Ray (1627–1705), *English Proverbs* (1670).

34. One white foot, buy him,
   Two white feet, try him;
   Three white feet, see how he goes,
   Four white feet, feed him to the crows.

anon.

35. One white foot—buy him;
   Two white feet—try him;
   Three white feet—look well about him;
   Four white feet—go without him.

Old English rhyme

36. A four white-foot horse is a horse for a fool;
   A three white-foot horse is a horse for a king;
   An if he hath but one, I'll give him to none.

James Howell (1594–1666), *English Proverbs* (1659).

37. One white foot, buy him,
   Two white feet, try him,
   Three white feet, deny him,
   Four white feet and a white nose,
   Take off his hide and feed him to the crows.

Harold W. Thompson (1891–1964),
Body, Boots and Britches (1940).

38. One white foot, keep him not a day,
Two white feet, send him soon away,
Three white feet, sell him to a friend,
Four white feet, keep him to the end.

Old English rhyme

39. Here were we fallen in a great question of the law, whether the grey mare may be the better horse or not.

Sir Thomas More (1478–1535), *Dialogue*, bk. 2, ch. 5 (1528).

40. The grey mare will prove the better horse.

Dutch proverb (1546)

41. The old grey mare, she ain't what she used to be.

American song (ca. 1880)

42. Lo, the Turquoise Horse of Johano-ai . . .
There he spurneth dust of glittering grains—
How joyous his neigh.

Navaho Song of the Horse

43. A specious and fantastic arrangement of words by which a man can prove a horse-chestnut to be a chestnut horse.

> Abraham Lincoln (1809–1865)
> speech (August 21, 1858) [referring to the tree,
> not the growth on a horse's leg], Ottawa, Illinois.

44. The sunshine's golden gleam is thrown,
On sorrel, chestnut, bay and roan.

> Oliver Wendell Holmes (1809–1894)

45. The old white horse is the end of all misfortune.

> Irish proverb

46. My purpose is, indeed, a horse of that color.

> William Shakespeare (1564–1616),
> *Twelfth Night*, act 2, sc. 3 (1599).

47. They are manifest asses but you, good Leech, you are a horse of another color.

> Richard Harris Barham [Thomas Ingoldsby]
> (1788–1845), *Leech of Folkestone*.

48. Farmer Gripper thinks we can live upon nothing, which is a horse of another color.

> C. H. Spurgeon (1834–1892),
> *John Ploughman's Pictures* (1880).

49. There's only one of 'em and he's it. He's the horse of a different color you've heard tell about.

"The Cabbie" [played by Frank Morgan (1890–1949)]
in *The Wizard of Oz* (1939); screenplay by Noel Langby (1911–1980),
Florence Ryerson (1894–) and Edgar Allan Woolf (d. 1943).

50. You can't judge a horse by its color.

anon.

51. A good horse is never a bad color.

anon.

52. There is no good horse of a bad color.

Izaak Walton (1593–1683),
The Compleat Angler, pt. 1, ch. 5 (1653).

53. A good horse is never of an ill color.

Samuel Palmer (d. 1732), *Moral Essays on Proverbs* (1710).

54. Horses are good of all hues.

James Kelly, *Scottish Proverbs* (1721).

55. Good horses can't be of a bad color.

Thomas Fuller (1654–1734), *Gnomologia* (1732).

56. "A good horse is never of an ill color" is wildly irreverent from the Oriental point of view.

J. L. Kipling (1837–1911), *Beast and Man* (1891).

57.   A bad horse is often a good color.

overheard (1989)

58.   The colour—grey or chestnut are the best, not white or dun.

Virgil (70–19 B.C.E.), *Georgics*, 3, 81 (30 B.C.E.).

59.   What horse? a roan? . . . That roan shall be my throne.
  Well, I will back him straight: O esperance!

William Shakespeare (1564–1616),
Henry IV, pt. 1, act 2, sc. 3 (1597).

60.   Black are the horses.
  The horseshoes are black.

Frederico García Lorca (1898–1936),
Romance de la Guardia Civil Española (1928).

61.   That's a grey horse of another color.

Octavus Roy Cohen (1891–1959), *May Day* (1929).

62.   An equine of a different color.

Bangor (ME) *Daily News*, July 18, 1958.

63.   That's a horse of a different feather.

Richard Lederer (1938–), *Anguished English* (1989).

64. They are strange horses, unlike any you have ever seen, for these horses sweat blood. And no other horses can compete with them; they are majestic in appearance and their hair is like silk and they are so clever they can understand what men are thinking and they are so strong they can gallop a thousand li in a day without any difficulty at all.

Chiang Ch'ien (d. 114 B.C.E.), envoy for
Chinese Emperor Wu Ti (156–87 B.C.E.)

65. The kick of a quiet horse strikes strong.

Armenian proverb

66. The horse can stand the horse's kick.

Pashto proverb

67. A kick from a mare never hurts a horse.

proverb

68. Never say "my horse doesn't kick."

Turki (Turfan) proverb

69. He is free of horses that never had one.

proverb

70. Ere twice the horses of the sun shall bring
Their firey torcher his diurnal ring.

William Shakespeare (1564–1616),
All's Well that Ends Well, act 2, sc. 1 (ca. 1602).

71. The rage for horses has become a positive
epidemic; many persons are infected with it
whom one would have credited with more sense.

Lucian (ca. 120–180)

72. A kingdom without horses was not a
kingdom, and a king without horses was not
a king.

Stan Steiner (1925–1985),
Dark and Dashing Horsemen (1981).

73. Of all animals kept for the recreation of
mankind the horse is
alone capable of exciting
a passion that shall be
absolutely hopeless.

Bret Harte (1836–1902)

74. To lie as fast as a horse can trot.

proverb

75. Horses are the opposite of dogs, gratitude-wise. You give a dog something totally wretched to eat, such as a toad part or a wad of pre-chewed Dentyne, and the dog will henceforth view you as the Supreme Being. . . . Whereas if you spend hours grooming a horse and lugging its food and water around, the horse will be thinking, "Should I chomp on this person's arm? Or should I merely blow a couple gallons of horse snot into this person's hair?"

Dave Barry (1947–), "Wit's End: Horsefeathers,"
in *The Washington Post Magazine*, July 28, 1991.

76. Where is the horse that doth untread again
His tedious measures with the unbated fire
That he did pace them first?

William Shakespeare (1564–1616),
The Merchant of Venice, act 2, sc. 6 (1596).

77. The only time a horse gets scared nowadays is when he meets another horse.

Will Rogers (1879–1935)

78. The only time a horse gets scared on the road nowadays is when he meets another horse.

Harry Oliver, *The Desert Rat Scrap Book*.

79. The horse, untamed, was dangerous. But it could be tamed. . . .

Michael Stapleton, *The Illustrated
Dictionary of Greek and Roman Mythology* (1978).

80. Horses for courses.

British proverb

81. Like human beings, horses are all individuals with singular personalities, their own virtues and their own faults. We become bound to them for their beauty, their eccentricities, their heart and the love they so often return to us.

Lana Slaton, *Horses in History Coloring Album* (1987).

82. I don't even like old cars . . . I'd rather have a goddam horse. A horse is at least human, for God's sake.

J. D. Salinger (1919–)

83. It is clear to everybody that the ordinary or nonprofessional horse ranks only with the dog as an animal likely to go to heaven. There are horses who never won anything, who never tried to win anything, who are remembered with love many years after their death, simply because they had ingratiating ways, stepped on some great bastard's foot and otherwise showed such decent character that no human could fail to love them.

Henry Mitchell (1923–1993), in
The Washington Post, June 9, 1989, sec. C.

84. What a colt learns, an old horse keeps.

Estonian proverb

85. Put no more on an old horse than he can bear.

David Garrick (1717–1779), May-Day, sc. 1 (1775).

86. An old horse does not forget his path.

Japanese proverb

87. What the colt learns in youth he continues in old age.

French proverb

88. An old horse won't spoil the furrows.

Russian proverb

89. As old wood is best to burn; old horses to ride; old books to read; old wine to drink, so are old friends always most trusty to use.

Leonard Wright (1555?–), *Display of Dutie* (1589).

90. Be wise in time, and turn loose the aging horse, lest at the last he stumble amid jeers and break his wind.

Horace (65–8 B.C.E.), *Epistles*, bk. 1, epistle 1 (ca. 20 B.C.E.).

91. Like the stout horse which oft has borne away
The prize, now, weak with age, he rest enjoys.

Quintus Ennius (ca. 239–169 B.C.E.), in
Cicero (106–43 B.C.E.), *de Senectute*, 5, 14 (ca. 45 B.C.E.).

92. However old the horse it is better than new sandals.

African (Hausa) proverb

93. When old horses get warm, they are not easily held in.

German proverb

94. The old horse must die in some man's hand.

Carmichaell (1628)

95. A good man will take care of his horses and dogs, when old and past service.

Plutarch (46–120)

96. What makes scholasticks degrade horses so much proceeds (I believe) from nothing else but the small knowledge they have of them, and from a persuasion that they themselves know everything.

William Cavendish, Marquis of Newcastle (1592–1676),
New Method of Dressing Horses (1667).

97. Live not in that city where no horse neighs, nor dog barks.

Indian (Hindi) proverb

98. The loose horse makes for his stall.

Asian proverb

99. A free horse is soon tired.

English proverb

100. The fast horse soon gets tired.

Slovakian proverb

101. If you possess a good horse it always becomes a gift.

Persian proverb

102. [They should be] blood bays, as large as possible, fine delicate heads, long necks, ears small and prick'd up near the ends, deep shoulders and chests, large arms, well legg'd, upright pasterns, clear of long hair, bodys good, loins round, and very wide, out hock'd, haunches straight and wide behind. There is something so striking and inexpressively beautiful in a fine horse.

Patrick Henry (1736–1799) letter (1779) to
Col. George Rogers Clark (1752–1818).

103. There are only two kinds of people in the world—those who own horses and those who wish they did.

Dale Robertson (1923–) on the 1970s
television show *American Horseman*

104. A horse is a horse, of course, of course . . .

Jay Livingston, theme to the 1960s
television show *Mister Ed* (1961–1965)

105. Wouldn't it be funny if it turned out that animals actually had high IQs and understood English perfectly, and the only reason they act stupid is that we're always giving them unintelligible commands? Like, maybe at night in the stable, the horses stand around asking each other "What the hell does 'giddyap' mean?"

Dave Barry (1947–), *Dave Barry Talks Back* (1991).

106. I compare thee my love to a steed of Pharoah's chariots.

Song of Solomon 1:9

107. Why tether your horse
    To a blossoming
cherry tree?
    As he prances
    The flowers will
flutter and fall.

Min-you,
Japanese folk song

108. In the event of a thunderstorm, the safest place is within a few feet of your horse, which being then a more elevated animal, will receive the shock in preference.

Old Farmer's Almanac (1800), in Hale, ed.,
The Best of the Old Farmer's Almanac (1991).

109. Most famous in our western and Indian traditions is that of the White Steed of the Prairies; a magnificent milk-white charger, large-eyed, small-headed, bluff-chested, and with the dignity of a thousand monarchs in his lofty, over-scorning carriage. He was the elected Xerxes of the vast herds of wild horses, whose pastures in those days were fenced only by the Rocky Mountains and the Alleghenies. At their flaming head he westward trooped it like the chosen star which each evening leads on the host of lights.

Herman Melville (1819–1891), *Moby Dick*, ch. 42 (1851).

110. How can the foal amble if the horse and the mare trot?

John Heywood (1497–1580), *Proverbs* (1564).

111.   The old horse learns not to amble.

Romanian proverb

112.   Hard is to teach an old horse amble true.

Edmund Spenser (1552–1599), The Fairie Queen,
bk. 3, canto 8, st. 26 (1589).

113.   The horse ambles according to his master.

Turkish proverb

114.   The horse does abominate the camel.

Increase Mather (1639–1723),
Remarkable Providences (1684).

115.   Horses (thou say'st) and asses men may try.
      And ring suspected vessels ere they buy.
      But wives, a random choice, untried they take,
      They dream in courtship, but in wedlock wake.

Geoffrey Chaucer (1340–1400), prologue to
"The Wife of Bath's Tale," The Canterbury Tales (1387).

116.   We stayed for you as one horse does for another.

Jonathan Swift (1678–1745), Polite Conversations (1738).

117.   We tolerate shapes in human beings that would horrify us if we saw them in a horse.

W. R. Inge (1860–1954)

118.   A short horse is soon curried.

John Heywood (1497–1580), *Proverbs* (1564).

119.   A little horse is soon curried.

James Howell (1594–1666), *Proverbs* (1659).

120.   A short horse is soon whisked.

James Kelly, *Scottish Proverbs* (1721).

121.   A short tale is soon told—and a short horse soon curried.

Sir Walter Scott (1771–1832), *The Abbot*, ch. 11 (1820).

122.   It don't take long to curry a short horse.

Johnson J. Hooper (1815–1862),
Adventures of Captain Simon Suggs (1854).

123.   Buy at three and sell at seven and you'll always have a good horse.

Irish proverb

124. A good horse finds a buyer even if it stops in the stable; a bad one has to be taken to fairs.

Czech proverb

125. He who has a good horse in his stable is not ashamed to go on foot.

Italian proverb

126. The wildest colts make the best horses.

Plutarch (46–120), *Parallel Lives: Life of Themistocles*.

127. Of a ragged colt there cometh a good horse.

John Heywood (1497–1580), *Proverbs* (1564).

128. Many a shabby colt makes a fine horse.

Irish proverb

129. A kindly colt will never make a good horse.

Scottish proverb

130. A wanton herd . . . of youthful and unhandled colts.

William Shakespeare (1564–1616),
The Merchant of Venice, act 5, sc. 1 (1596).

131. Young hot colts being raged do rage the more.

William Shakespeare (1564–1616),
Richard II, act 2, sc. 1 (1595).

132. As nervous as a colt.

proverb

133. Then I beat my tabor;
       At which, like unback'd colts, they prick'd
their ears,
       Advanced their eyelids, lifted up their noses
       As they smelt music. . . .

William Shakespeare (1564–1616),
The Tempest, act 4, sc. 1 (1610).

134. There is no colt but will break some halter.

English proverb

135. No foal in India, no tabby cat in China, nor
lion's cub in Teheran.

Persian proverb

136. When you have brandy and keep yourself
half drunk, you can go through the winter like
a horse.

English Romany proverb

137. There is just as much horse sense as ever, but
the horses have most of it.

anon.

138. I don't think I ever knew a horse more lacking in—well, horse sense.

Michael Innes [John Innes Mackintosh Stewart] (1906–?), *Daffodil Affair* (1942).

139. You don't want a flighty idiotic horse; you want an even-tempered one with a lot of . . . horse-sense.

Glen Randall, in Rothel, *The Great Show Business Animals* (1980).

140. Good horse sense is that sense that horses have, never to bet on human beings.

Alan Gregg (1890–1957), *For Future Doctors, Creativeness in Medicine* (1957).

141. With flowing tail and flying mane,
With nostrils never stretch'd by pain,
Mouths bloodless to the bit or rein;
And feet that iron never shod,
And flanks unscar'd by spur or rod,
A thousand horse—the wild—the free—
Like waves that follow o'er the sea—
Came thickly thundering on.

George Gordon, Lord Byron (1788–1824), *Mazeppa* (1819).

142. Honor lies in the mane of a horse.

Arabic proverb

143. The stable wears out a horse more than the road.

French proverb

144. The borrowed horse has hard hoofs.

Irish proverb

145. With a borrowed horse you use your spurs.

Mexican-American proverb

146. A borrowed horse and your own spurs make short miles.

Danish and German proverb

147. On a borrowed horse you cannot travel far.

Russian proverb

148. Forgive a horse that will cock his ears.

Irish proverb

149. It is difficult to tie an unborn horse to the manger.

Danish proverb

150. Who does not venture gets neither horse nor mule; and who ventures too much loses horse and mule.

French proverb

151. In real life we are content with oats that are really middling, are very glad to have a useful horse, and know that if we drink port at all, we must drink some that is neither good nor sound.

Anthony Trollope (1815–1882),
The Eustace Diamonds, ch. 35 (1837).

152. Poverty is owning a horse.

1980s bumper sticker

153. Poverty is owning horses.

1990s bumper sticker

154. Fair words buy horses on credit.

Trinidad proverb

155. Horses and hounds devour their masters.

John Clarke (1609–1676) [economically speaking],
Paroemiologia (1639).

156. Eaten up by horses.

> Juvenal (40–125) [referring to the cost of keeping horses],
> *Satires*, sat. 11 (ca. 120).

157. A running horse is an open grave.

> John Florio (1553–1625),
> *First Fruites*, fo. 28 (1578).

158. There are unknown worlds of knowledge in brutes; and whenever you mark a horse, or a dog, with a peculiarly mild, calm, deep-seated eye, be sure he is an Aristotle or a Kant, tranquilly speculating upon the mysteries in man.

> Herman Melville (1819–1891),
> *Redburn*, ch. 40 (1849).

159. No philosophers so thoroughly comprehend us as dogs and horses.

> Herman Melville (1819–1891), *Redburn*, ch. 40 (1849).

160. A horse is once a foal; man is a child twice in his lifetime.

> Czech proverb

161. Why can't an investigating committee show a grain of common sense? If I send a man to buy a horse for me, I expect him to tell me that horse's points—not how many hairs he has in his tail.

Abraham Lincoln (1809–1865), in Sandburg,
*Abraham Lincoln: The Prairie Years
and the War Years*, ch. 34 (1954).

162. A man, a horse and a dog never weary of each other's company.

eighteenth-century proverb

163. Champing his foam and bounding o'er
the plain,
Arch his high neck, and graceful spread
his mane.

Sir Richard Blackmore (1650–1729)

164. His screaming stallions maned with whistling wind.

Anna Hempsted Branch (1875–1937),
Nimrod With the Angels (1910).

165. They cannot set their horses in the same stable.

John Clarke (1609–1676) [when people disagree],
Paroemiologia (1639).

166. It's an ill jade can neither whinny nor wag his tail.

unknown, *Maroccus Extaticus* (1595).

167. It's an ill horse can neither whinny nor wag his tail.

John Clarke (1609–1676), *Paroemiologia* (1639); also John Ray (1627–1705), *English Proverbs* (1670).

168. It is a silly horse, that can neither whinny, nor wag his tail.

Thomas Fuller (1654–1734), *Gnomologia*, no. 2882 (1732).

169. To a weary horse even his own tail is a burden.

Czech proverb

170. It is hair by hair that the horse grows bob-tailed.

Welsh proverb

171. Every horse scares the flies away with its own tail.

Italian proverb

172. She carries her tail high, as all well-bred
Arabians do, and there is a neatness and finish
about every movement, which remind one of a
fawn or a gazelle. We are all agreed that she is
incomparably superior to anything we have seen
here or elsewhere and would be worth a king's
ransom, if kings were still worth ransoming.

Lady Anne Blunt (1837–1917), in *Arabian Horse World*
vol. 25, no. 12 (September 1985): 454.

173. Spare is her head and lean.
Her ears pricked close together . . .
Her neck curved like a palm branch,
Her forehead like a lamp lighted,
Her withers clean and sharp . . .
Her forelegs are twin lances.
Her hooves fly ever faster
Than flies the whirlwind,
Her tail bone held aloft,
Yet the hairs sweep the gravel;
Her height twice eight, sixteen,
Taller than all the horses. . . .

unknown; an Arab's description of Agheyli Jaber's
world-renowned grey mare, *Arabian Horse World*
vol. 25, no. 12 (September 1985): 449.

174. Visual analysis tells you what an Arabian horse appears to be. Pedigree tells you what he should be. Progeny tells you what he actually is.

Yochanan Merchav, in *Arabian Horse World* vol. 27, no. 3 (December 1986): 314.

175. The only pure breed is the Arab, which is unique.

E. Hartley Edwards (1927–), *The Ultimate Horse Book* (1991).

176. My beautiful, my beautiful! That standest meekly by,
   With thy proudly-arched and glossy neck, and dark and firey eye!

Caroline Sheridan Norton (1808–1877), *The Arab's Farewell to his Steed*.

177. Gamarra is a dainty steed,
   Strong, black, and of a noble breed,
   Full of fire, and full of bone,
   With all his line of fathers known;
   Fine his nose, his nostrils thin,

But blown abroad by
the pride within;
His mane is like a
river flowing,
And his eyes like
embers glowing
In the darkness of
the night,
And his pace as swift as light.

Barry Cornwall (1787–1874), *An Arab Blood-Horse*, st. 1.

178. Hobby horses are dearer than Arabians.

German proverb

179. The Arabian horse is . . . the most beautiful
of all.

E. Hartley Edwards (1927–),
The Ultimate Horse Book (1991).

180. They could turn on a dime and give you
back nine cents change.

saying about the Quarter Horse

181. Three things are men most likely to be cheated in, a horse, a wig, and a wife.

Benjamin Franklin (1706–1790),
Poor Richard's Almanak (1736).

182. Three things are not to be trusted—a cow's horns, a dog's tooth, and a horse's hoof.

P. W. Joyce (1827–1914),
English as We Speak It (1910).

183. Trust not a horse's heels, nor a dog's tooth.

John Ray (1627–1705), *English Proverbs* (1670).

184. From the heels of a horse keep at a distance.

Henderson, *Latin Proverbs* (ca. 500).

185. Stay away from a horse's heels.

Erasmus (1466–1536), *Adagia*, ch. 1 (1523).

186. Beware of an ox before, a horse behind, and a monk all around.

anon.

187. Fear the goat from the front, the horse from the rear, and man from all sides.

Russian proverb

188. He's mad that trusts in the tameness of a wolf, a horse's health, a boy's love, or a whore's oath.

William Shakespeare (1564–1616),
King Lear, act 3, sc. 6 (1605).

189. Don't trust a horse on the road or a wife at home.

Yiddish folk saying

190. The son of a widow who has cattle, the foal of an old mare at grass, and the dog of a miller who has meal, are the three merriest creatures living.

Irish proverb

191. In this world only three things dispel anxiety: women, horses, and books.

Arabic proverb

192. Three things prolong life—a big house, a swift horse and an obedient wife.

Arabic proverb

193. Blood's the word. Nothing like blood, in hosses, dawgs, and men.

William Makepeace Thackeray (1811–1863),
Vanity Fair (1847–1848).

194. When a valet preaches at table and a horse grazes in the ford, it is time to take them away, for they have stayed long enough.

Le Ménagier de Paris,
A Medieval Home Companion,
ed. and trans. Tania Bayard (1991).

195. He will hold thee, when his passion shall have spent its novel force,
  Something better than his dog, a little dearer than his horse.

Alfred, Lord Tennyson (1809–1892),
Locksley Hall (1842).

196. Where the horse lieth down, there some hairs will be found.

Thomas Fuller (1608–1661), *History of the
Worthies of England*, vol. 1 (1662).

197. Where the horse rolls itself it leaves some of its hair.

Welsh proverb

198. Where the horse wallows the hair remains behind.

Finnish proverb

199.   Show me a man who has no pity on his horse, and I will show you one who is a cruel husband, if he is married, and a tyrannical parent, if he has children; a man that would be a Nero if he had the power. He is a coward by nature and a fiend by practice.

George Eliot (1819–1889),
Middlemarch, bk. 8 (1872).

200. If coroner's inquests sat on horses, those doctors would be found guilty of mareslaughter.

George Meredith (1829–1909),
The Ordeal of Richard Feverel, 24 (1859).

201.   The horses of hope gallop, but the asses of experience go slowly.

Russian proverb

202. Oats: a grain which in England is generally given to horses, but in Scotland supports the people.

Samuel Johnson (1709–1784),
Dictionary (1755).

203. Horses and poets should be fed, not overfed.

Charles IX of France (1550–1574)

204. While the grass groweth, the horse starveth.

John Heywood (1497–1580), *Proverbs* (1564).

205. A horse is not caught with an empty sack.

Turkish proverb

206. Even if a horse is fed with sweets and bread, it will still prefer its hay.

Philippine proverb

207. The horse must graze where it is tethered.

Flemish proverb

208. Empty stalls make biting horses.

Scottish proverb

209. Soft grass for an old horse.

Bulgarian proverb

210. Nothing fattens the horse so well as the master's eye.

Greek proverb

211. The best feed of a horse is his master's eye.

Spanish proverb

212. The horse fed too liberally with oats becomes unruly.

The Talmud

213. He who advises you to buy a horse with a big belly will not help you feed him.

Haitian proverb

214. A common horse is always lean.

Lithuanian proverb

215. A horse will not avoid oats.

English proverb

216. The sky is high, and the horses fatten.

Japanese proverb

217. Two of the horse's worst enemies are fat and rest.

Kerry Ridgway, D.V.M., in *Arabian Horse World* vol. 26, no. 11 (August 1986).

218. A bad horse eats as much as a good one.

Danish proverb

219. A jade eats as much as a good horse.

George Herbert (1593–1633),
Jacula Prudentum, no. 521 (1640).

220. A bad horse eats as much as a good one—and sometimes more.

Nancy Evans (March 1989)

221. To a greedy eating horse a short halter.

George Herbert (1593–1633),
Jacula Prudentum, no. 1104 (1640).

222. Live, horse! and thou shalt have grass.

Jonathan Swift (1667–1745),
Polite Conversation (1738).

223. The leaner the horse, the less kicking he does.

Italian proverb

224. Colt in de barley-patch kick high.

Joel Chandler Harris (1848–1908),
Uncle Remus: Plantation Proverbs (1880).

225. A horse grown fat kicks.

Italian proverb

226. It is a poor horse that is not worth his oats.

Danish proverb

227. It's a very proud horse that will not carry his oats.

Italian proverb

228. The horse must go to the manger, and not the manger to the horse.

Danish proverb

229. A hungry horse makes a clean manger.

James Howell (1594–1666), *English Proverbs* (1650).

230. It is unreasonable to expect a horse should void oats which never eats any.

Benjamin Franklin (1706–1790), *Works* (1745).

231. If the horse did not blow on its oats it would swallow a lot of dust.

Russian proverb

232. When the horse is starved you bring him oats.

English proverb

233. Where the horse is tied, there it feeds.

Philippine proverb

234. The ox plows the field, and the horse eats the grain.

Chinese proverb

235. It is a bad horse that does not earn his fodder.

German proverb

236. A good horse is worth his fodder.

Dutch proverb

237. The old horse may die waiting for new grass.

proverb

238. The old horse must die in someone's keeping.

proverb

239. A horse will see the corn but not the fence.

Welsh proverb

240. As hungry as a horse.

saying

241. What is grass to the lion is flesh to the horse.

Turkish proverb

242. If two men feed a horse, it will be thin; if two men fix a boat, it will leak.

Chinese proverb

243. When the manger is empty the horses fight.

Danish proverb

244. Better a lean jade than an empty halter.

Thomas Fuller (1654–1734), *Gnomologia*, no. 863 (1732).

245. Better a poor horse than an empty stall.

Danish proverb

246. Better the horse that is on its way than the one in its stall.

Welsh proverb

247. Who buys a horse buys care.

Spanish proverb

248. In a wind horses and cows do not agree.

Chinese proverb

249. To see his sweet looks, and hear her sweet words . . . it would have made a horse break his halter sure.

John Heywood (1497–1580), *Proverbs* (1564).

250. It would make a horse break his halter, to see so drunken a pageant.

> Richard Stanyhurst (1547–1618),
> *A Description of Ireland*, fo. 6 (1577).

251. You can have it straight from the horse's mouth.

> Francis Isles [Anthony Berkeley Cox] (1893–1932),
> *Before the Fact*, ch. 16 (1932).

252. That's official, from the horse's mouth. Or the horse's arse.

> Julian Symons (1912–),
> *The Plot Against Roger Rider* (1973).

253. A one-horse place.

> proverb

254. A scabbed horse abides no comb.

> John Davies (1565–1618), *Scourge of Folly* (1611).

255. If any of you get cross over it, I shall tell you that sore horses cannot bear to be combed.

> C. H. Spurgeon (1834–1892),
> *John Ploughman's Talk*, ch. 3 (1869).

256. A galled horse does not care to be curried.

French proverb

257. From the horse to the ass.

Procopius (499–565) [from better to worse],
Anecdota (ca. 526).

258. A handsome horse should have a head like a maiden, a chest like a widow, and a foot like a baby.

Polish proverb

259. [A] horse should have eighteen characteristics. Three qualities of a fox: short, straight ears; good hair; and a strong tail full of hair. Four qualities of a hare: a lean head; extreme wariness; light movement, and speed. Four qualities of an ox: a wide, large and broad chest; a large belly; large eyes that stand out from the head; and low jointedness. Three qualities of an ass: good feet; a strong backbone; and gentleness. Four qualities of a maiden: a beautiful mane; a beautiful chest; beautiful loins; and large buttocks.

Le Ménagier de Paris, *A Medieval Home Companion*,
ed. and trans. Tania Bayard (1991).

260. The horse is distinguished by six characteristics: it is wanton; delights in the strife of war; is high-spirited; despises sleep; eats much; voids little.

Pesachim 113b

261. A good horse should have three propyrtees of a man, three of a woman, three of a foxe, three of a hare, and three of an asse:

Of a man. Bolde, prowde, and hardye.

Of a Woman. Fayre-breasted, fair of hair, and easy to move.

Of a foxe. A fair taylle, short ears, with a good trot.

Of a hare. A grate eye, a dry head, and well rennynge.

Of an asse. A bygge chynn, a flat legge, and a good hoof.

Wynkyn de Worde (1496) (d. 1534?)

262. How now? Whose mare's dead, what's the matter?

William Shakespeare (1564–1616),
Henry IV, pt. 2, act 2, sc. 1 (1597).

263. The man shall have his mare again, and all shall be well.

William Shakespeare
(1564–1616),
A Midsummer Night's Dream,
act 3, sc. 2 (1595).

264. He smiles like a brewer's horse.

English proverb

265. As melancholy as a collier's horse.

English proverb

266. Why brook'st thou, ignorant horse, subjection?

John Donne (1572–1631),
Holy Sonnets, 12 (1617).

267. As fit as a horse.

proverb

268. A heart as big as a horse.

W. Mankowitz (1924–), *Old* (1956).

269. To sweat like a horse.

proverb

270. There is a common saying that says, he hath as many diseases as a horse, but 'tis false, for man hath many more.

James Howell (1594–1666), *Parly of Beasts* (1660).

271. As sick as a horse.

proverb

272. A cough will stick longer by a horse than a peck of oats.

British proverb

273. Sickness comes on horseback and departs on foot.

Dutch proverb

274. Agues come on horseback, but go away on foot.

English proverb

275. Diseases come on couriers' horses, but go away on tired oxen.

Estonian proverb

276. Diseases come swift as horses and go back slow as lice.

Indian (Sindhi) proverb

277. Misfortune arrives on horseback but departs on foot.

Polish proverb

278. Have a horse of your own, and you may borrow another.

James Howell (1594–1666), *British Proverbs* (1659).

279. My horse has a hoof like a striped agate,
His fetlock is like a fine eagle plume, His legs are like lightning.

My horse's body is like an arrow of eagle feathers.

My horse has a tail like a thin black cloud.
The Holy Wind blows through his mane,
His mane is made of rainbows.
My horse's ears are made of round corn.
My horse's eyes are made of stars.

Navaho horse song

280. They excelled the snows in whiteness, the
gales in speed.

Virgil (70–19 B.C.E.), *Aeneid*, bk. 12 (19 B.C.E.).

281. Their horses were of great stature, strong and
clean-limbed; their grey coats glistened, their long
tails flowed in the wind, their manes were braided
on their proud necks.

J.R.R. Tolkien (1892–1973),
The Lord of the Rings, pt. 2,
The Two Towers, rev. ed. (1965).

282. . . . tireless, swift as the flowing wind.
Shadowfax they called him. By day his coat
glistens like silver; and by night it is like a shade,
and he passes unseen. Light is his footfall!

J.R.R. Tolkien (1892–1973),
The Lord of the Rings, pt. 1,
The Fellowship of the Ring, rev. ed. (1965).

283. Round-hoof'd, short-jointed, fetlocks shag
and long,
    Broad breast, full eye, small head and nostril
wide,
    High crest, short ears, straight legs and
passing strong,
    Thin mane, thick tail, broad buttock, tender hide:

Look, what a horse
should have he did not
lack,
  Save a proud rider
on so proud a back.

William Shakespeare
(1564–1616),
Venus and Adonis (1592).

284. The horse was of extraordinary size, with a lofty neck, bay in color, with a thick, glossy mane; but that same horse was of such a fate or fortune, that whomever possessed it came to utter ruin, as well as his whole house and all his possessions.

Aulus Gellius (117–180),
Noctes Atticae, bk. 3, ch. 9 (150).

285. That man has the horse of Sejanus.

Aulus Gellius (117–180) , *Noctes Atticae*, bk. 3, ch. 9 (150)
[proverbial phrase for an unlucky person;
the horse of Sejanus is described in quotation 284].

286. Cob was the strongest, Mob was the wrongest, Chittabob's tail was the finest and longest!

Richard Harris Barham
[Thomas Ingoldsby] (1788–1845),
The Truants.

287. She was iron-sinew'd and satin-skinned,
Ribbed like a drum and limb'd like a deer,
Fierce as the fire and fleet as the wind—
There was nothing she couldn't climb
or clear.

A. L. Gordon (1833–1870),
The Romance of Britomarte.

288. It is a most absolute and excellent horse.

William Shakespeare (1564–1616),
Henry V, act 3, sc. 7 (1598).

289. His neck is high and erect, his head replete
with intelligence, his belly short, his back full,
and his proud chest swells with hard muscle.

Virgil (70–19 B.C.E.),
Georgics, bk. 3 (30 B.C.E.).

290. Hast thou given the horse strength? Hast thou
clothed his neck with thunder?

Job 39:19

291. Men are not hanged for stealing horses, but that horses may not be stolen.

Marquis of Halifax (1633–1695),
Political Thoughts and Reflections, on Punishment.

292. When the horse has been stolen, the fool shuts the stable.

French proverb (ca. 1303)

293. It was only shutting the stable door after the steed was stolen.

Daniel Defoe (1660–1731), *Robinson Crusoe* (1719).

294. When the steed is stolen, shut the stable door.

John Heywood (1497–1580), *Proverbs* (1564).

295. When steedes are stolne tys bootles doores to barre.

George Turberville (1540–1610),
Tragical Tales (1587).

296. When the stede is stolyn to shyt the stable dore Comys small pleasoure profyte or vaintage.

Alexander Barclay (1475–1552),
The Shyp of Folys (1508).

297. When the hors is stole stake the stabull-dore.

anon., *Douce MS* (ca. 1350).

298. Country folk have a saying: Too late to close the stable when the horse is lost.

anon., *Li Proverb au Vilain* (ca. 1190).

299. Seldom does thief ride home to the stable.

J.R.R. Tolkien (1892–1973),
The Lord of the Rings, pt. 2,
The Two Towers, rev. ed. (1965).

300. A horse gallops with his lung, perseveres with his heart, and wins with his character.

Frederico Tesio, in Isenbart and Bührer,
The Kingdom of the Horse (1969).

301. Sell the cow, buy the sheep, but never be without the horse.

Irish proverb

302. Don't refuse to sell your horse for the sake of a crown.

Irish proverb

303. Nothing so bold as a blind mare.

Scottish proverb

304. He has chang'd his one ey'd horse for a blind one.

Benjamin Franklin (1706–1790),
Poor Richard's Almanack (1733).

305. Bline hoss don't fall w'en he follers de bit.

Joel Chandler Harris (1848–1908),
Uncle Remus: Plantation Proverbs (1880).

306. Mettle is dangerous in a blind horse.

John Ray (1627–1705), *English Proverbs* (1680).

307. One stiff blind horse, his every bone astare,
Stood stupified, however he came there:
Thrust out past service from the devil's stud!

Robert Browning (1812–1889),
Childe Roland to the Dark Tower Came.

308. The blind horse is the hardiest.

John Ray (1627–1705), *Proverbs: Scottish* (1678).

309. The blind horse is fittest for the mill.

Thomas Southerne (1660–1746),
Maid's Last Prayer, act 3, sc. 1 (1693).

310. Better a blind horse than an empty halter.

Danish proverb; also Dutch proverb

311. The blind nag goes straight ahead.

German proverb

312. Nothing so bold as a blind horse.

Greek proverb

313. As wary as a blind horse.

Thomas Fuller (1654–1734), *Gnomologia* (1732).

314. A nod is as good as a wink to a blind horse.

proverb

315. A bold man makes a bold horse.

proverb

316. To cleanse the Augean stables.

proverb [meaning to do the impossible]

317. The best horse needs breaking, and the aptest child needs teaching.

John Clarke (1609–1676),
Paroemiologia (1639);
also Thomas Fuller (1654–1734),
Gnomologia, no. 6441 (1732).

318. The best horse needs a whip, the wisest man advice, and the chastest woman a man.

Yiddish proverb

319. The horse that draws after him his halter, is not altogether escaped.

George Herbert (1593–1633),
Jacula Prudentum, no. 1118 (1640).

320. The speed of a runaway horse counts for nothing.

Jean Cocteau (1889–1963)

321. Zeal without knowledge is a runaway horse.

proverb

322. A runaway horse punishes himself.

Italian proverb

323. An inch of a nag is worth a span of an aver [a work-horse].

David Ferguson, *Scottish Proverbs* (1595).

324. An inch of a horse is worth a span of a colt.

Thomas Fuller (1654–1734),
Gnomologia, no. 636 (1732).

325. Even horses die from work.

Russian proverb

326. Strong as a horse.

proverb

327. You may break a horse's back, be he ever
so strong.

John Clarke (1609–1676), *Paroemiologia* (1639).

328. It is the last feather which breaks the
horse's back.

English proverb

329. Strong as a Flanders mare.

anon.

330. Patience is a strong horse, but it tires at last.

proverb

331. To sing psalms to a dead horse.

unknown [referring to an exercise in futility]

332. You're whipping a dead horse.

Titus Maccius Plautus (254–154 B.C.E.),
Pseudolus (ca. 195 B.C.E.).

333. To flog a dead horse.

proverb

334. It's no use to flog a dead horse.

Richard Chenevix Trench (1807–1886),
Lectures in Medieval Church History (1879).

335. Publishers don't believe in flogging a dead horse, but they concur in using the whip on a running horse.

New York Times Book Review (March 24, 1957).

336. Mingle the good with the bad, as men say,
let the quick horse draw the dead horse out of
the mire.

William Bullein (d. 1576),
A Dialogue Against the Fever Pestilence (1573)
["quick" means "live" or "living"].

337. His land . . . 'twas sold to pay his debts;
All went that way, for a dead horse, as one
would say.

Richard Brome (d. 1652),
The Antipodes, act 1 (1638).

338. To work for a dead horse. To work out an
old debt, or without hope of future reward.

John Ray (1627–1705), *English Proverbs* (1670).

339. He is working for a dead horse.

Zulu proverb

340. The best horse is just a carcass when it dies.

Yiddish proverb

341. Men will keep going on their nerve or
their head,
But you cannot ride a horse when he's dead.

Leonard Bacon (1887–1954), *Colorado Morton's Ride*.

342. Stop beating a dead horse to death.

Richard Lederer (1938–), *Anguished English* (1989).

343. While the grass grows, the horse dies.

Simone Teatino, *Epigram* (ca. 1238).

344. That was how his life happened.
No mad hooves galloping in the sky,
But the weak, washy way of true tragedy—
A sick horse nosing around the meadow for
a clean place to die.

Patrick Kavanaugh (1905–1967),
Soul For Sale: The Great Hunger (1947).

345. Dogs never go into mourning, when a
horse dies.

Thomas Fuller (1654–1734),
Gnomologia, no. 1314 (1732).

346. The horse dies and leaves his tail in the world.

Yoruba proverb

347. The horse died years ago . . . we've been
flogging him like mad and he hasn't twitched a
muscle.

Alan Hunter (1922–), *Gently Sahib* (1964).

348. There is no sense flogging a willing horse.

> Victor Bridges (1878–1972), *The Red Lodge* (1924).

349. Take horses. You can always believe a horse. I always say to everybody, Give me a horse, and I'll believe it.

> T. H. White (1915–1986),
> *Mistress Masham's Repose*, ch. 28 (1946).

350. The horse bit the parson!
>>How came it to pass?
>The horse heard the parson say,
>>"All flesh is grass."

> H. J. Loaring, *Epitaphs, Quaint,
> Curious and Elegant* (1872).

351. A fence lasts three years; a dog, three fences; a horse, three dogs; a man, three horses.

> German proverb

352. A fence should be horse high, hog tight, bull strong.

> F. F. Gould, *New York
> Times Magazine* (August 12, 1956).

353. Horse at home; price in market.

Indian (Hindi) proverb

354. Bring on the empty horses!

Michael Curtiz (1888–1962), in Niven,
Bring on the Empty Horses, ch. 6 (1975).

355. Be ye not as the horse or the mule, which have no understanding.

Psalms 32:9

356. What the horses o' Kansas think today, the horses of America will think tomorrow; an' I tell you that when the horses of America rise in their might, the day o' the oppressor is ended.

Rudyard Kipling (1865–1936),
"A Walking Delegate," in *The Day's Work* (1898).

357. There is nothing better for the inside of a man than the outside of a horse.

Will Rogers (1879–1935), among others

358. There is nothing so good for the inside of a man as the outside of a horse.

John Henry Temple,
Lord Palmerston (1784–1865), among others

359. Nothing does as much for the insides of a man as the outsides of a horse.

Ronald Reagan (1911–)

360. The glory of his snorting is terrible. He paws in the valley, and rejoices in his strength. . . . He swallows the ground with storm and rage. . . . He smells the battle afar off.

Job 39:20–21, 24–25

361. Henceforth the mares demand the greater care.

When in the course of the months they are in foal,

Allow them not to gallop in the swirling floods,

But let them graze in the glades by brimming streams.

Virgil (70–19 B.C.E.)

362. A whip for the horse, a bridle for the ass, and a rod for the back of fools.

Proverbs 26:10

363. The parson's horse was as lean, and as lank, and as sorry a jade as Humility herself could have bestrided.

Laurence Sterne (1713–1768),
Tristram Shandy, I (1760–1767).

364. Dangerous at both ends and uncomfortable in the middle.

Ian Fleming (1908–1964),
in *The Sunday Times* (London),
October 9, 1966.

365. The flies go to lean horses.

James Sanford (fl. 1567),
Hours of Recreation (1572).

366. A man may well bring a horse to the water,
But he cannot make him drink without he will.

John Heywood (1497–1580), *Proverbs* (1564).

367. Talk about bringing a horse to the water, we've brought the water to the horse.

H. H. Munro (1870–1916), The Square Egg (1924).

368. A man may lead a horse to the water, but he'll choose to drink.

unknown, *Jack Drum*, act 1 (1616).

369. You may bring a horse to river, but he will drink when and what he pleaseth.

George Herbert (1593–1633),
Jacula Prudentum (1640).

370. It extended only so far as bringing the horse to water. There appeared to be innumerable reasons why he should not drink.

George Douglas Howard Cole (1889–1959),
Murder at Crome House (1927).

371. One may lead a horse to water, but twenty cannot make him drink.

Samuel Johnson (1709–1784),
in Boswell, *Life of Johnson* (1763).

372. She not only led the horse to water but was able to make him drink against his will.

S. L. Bradbury, *Hiram* (1936).

373. You can lead a horse to water . . . if he's thirsty.

Hank Ketchum (1920–), "Dennis the Menace"
comic strip, in *The Washington Post*, January 5, 1992.

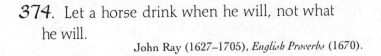

374. Let a horse drink when he will, not what he will.

John Ray (1627–1705), English Proverbs (1670).

375. Who may water that horse which will not drink?

unknown, Lambeth Homilies (ca. 1175).

376. You can lead a horse to water, but even he won't drink the stuff.

Phoebe Atwood Taylor (1890–1976),
Figure Away (1937).

377. It is hard to water a horse which does not hold down his head.

Finnish proverb

378. Who is he that may water the horse and not drink himself?

unknown, Old English Homilies, series 1 (ca. 1175).

379. You may force a horse to the water, but you cannot make him drink.

Danish proverb

380. You can lead a horse to water; you may be able to make him drink; you sure as hell can't expect the horse to thank you.

Edith Lathen [pseud. for Martha Hennissart and Mary Jane Latsis], *Sweet and Low* (1974).

381. A hungry dog and a thirsty horse pay no heed to blows.

Danish proverb

382. Where in all the world is nobility found without conceit? Where is there friendship without envy? Where is beauty without vanity? Here one finds gracefulness coupled with power, and strength tempered with gentleness. A constant servant, yet no slave. A fighter, ever without hostility. Our history was written on his back. We are his heirs. But he is his own heritage, the horse.

H.-H. Isenbart (1923–?), in Isenbart and Bührer, *The Kingdom of the Horse* (1969).

383. Hold your horses.

proverb

384. The horse appears to be content with as few ideas as a domestic animal can well have.

Leigh Hunt (1784–1899), *The Indicator* (1881).

385. 'Orses and dorgs is some men's fancy. They're wittles and drink to me—lodging, wife and children—reading, writing, and 'rithmetic— snuff, tobaker, and sleep.

Charles Dickens (1812–1870), *David Copperfield* (1849–1850).

386. Care, and not fine stables, makes a good horse.

Danish proverb

387. The horse is flesh and blood on a noble scale.

Jeff Griffen, *The Book of Horses and Horsemanship* (1963).

388. And some are sulky, while some will plunge.
Some you must gentle and some you must lunge.
Some—there are losers in every trade—
Will break their hearts ere bitted and made,
Will fight like fiends as the rope cuts hard,
And die dumb-mad in the breaking-yard.

Rudyard Kipling (1865–1936),
"Horses," in *Plain Tales From the Hills* (1934).

389. Visions of horses . . . make the moment brighter, inspire respect, and make the heart beat faster.

The Founders of The Sunshine Horse Lovers Club (1991)

390. If a horse had anything to say, he would speak up.

Jewish proverb

391. If a horse realized how small a man is, it would trample him at once.

Jewish proverb

392. It is beautiful to watch a fine horse gallop, the long stride, the rush of the wind as he passes—my heart beats quicker to the thud of the hoofs and I feel his strength. Gladly would I have the strength of the Tartar stallion roaming the wild steppe, the very strength, what vehemence of soul-thought would accompany it.

Richard Jeffries (1848–1887), *The Story of My Heart* (1883).

393. Without a horse and a dog and a friend, a man would perish.

Rudyard Kipling (1865–1936), "On the Great Wall," in *Puck of Pook's Hill* (1906).

394. Time's horses gallop down the lessening hill.

Richard Le Gallienne (1866–1947), *Time Flies*.

395. Yet if man, of all the Creator planned,
His noblest work is reckoned,
Of the works of His hand, by sea or by land,
The horse may at least rank second.

A. L. Gordon (1833–1879), *Hippodromania*, pt. 1, st. 3.

396. [Horses] were the celestial spaceships of ancient religions.

Stan Steiner (1925–1985), *Dark and Dashing Horsemen* (1981).

397. And God took a handful of southerly wind, blew his breath over it, and created the horse.

Bedouin legend

398. The air of heaven is that which blows between the horse's ears.

Arabic proverb

399. God forbid that I should go to any heaven in which there are no horses.

Robert Bontine Cunninghame-Graham (1852–1936)
letter to Theodore Roosevelt (1917)

400. Prayers to the horse's ears.

Japanese proverb

401. If cattle and horses, or lions, had hands, or were able to draw with their feet and produce the works which men do, horses would draw the forms of gods like horses, and cattle like cattle, and they would make the gods' bodies the same shape as their own.

Xenophanes (570–475 B.C.E.), Fragment 15.

402. When God created the horse he said to the magnificent creature: I have made thee as no other. All the treasures of the earth shall lie between thy eyes. Thou shalt cast thy enemies between thy hooves, but thou shalt carry my friends upon thy back. Thy saddle shall be the seat of prayers to me. And thou fly without any wings, and conquer without any sword. Oh, horse.

The Koran

403. An horse is a vain thing for safety.

Psalms 33:17

404. A horse thou knowest, a man thou dost not know.

Alfred, Lord Tennyson (1809–1892),
Gareth and Lynette (1872).

405. And the hoofs of the horses as they run shake the crumbling field.

Virgil (70–19 B.C.E.), *Aeneid*, bk. 11 (19 B.C.E.).

406. Whose laughs are hardy, tho' his jests are coarse,
    And who loves you best of all things—but his horse.

Alexander Pope (1688–1744),
*Epistle to Mrs. Teresa Blount
on Her Leaving Town* (1714).

407. Shoe the horse, shoe the mare, but let the little colt go bare.

anon., *Shoe the Horse*

408. Speedy horses cast the most shoes.

Swiss proverb

409. One can't shoe a running horse.

Dutch proverb

410. Evermore the common horse is worst shod.

John Heywood (1497–1580), *Proverbs* (1564).

411. It is a good horse that never stumbles.

John Ray (1627–1705), English Proverbs (1670).

412. A horse may stumble, though he has four feet.

Dutch proverb

413. A horse has four legs and even he stumbles.

Russian proverb

414. Let me say three things which shall become proverbs after my death: the best of horses may stumble, the best sword rebound without cutting, the best of men may commit a fault.

Al Hillale (ca. 100),
in Ibn Khallikan, *Deaths of Eminent Men*.

415. A horse may stumble on four feet.

John Ray (1627–1705), *Proverbs: Scottish* (1678).

416. A mare that is shod slips.

French proverb

417. Be a horse ever so well shod, he may slip.

French proverb

418. Stumbling is the excuse of the lame horse.

Hindu proverb

419. A horse with four feet may snapper [stumble] by a time.

James Kelly, *Scottish Proverbs* (1721).

420. 'Tis the horse that stumbles, not the saddle.

Thomas Fuller (1654–1734),
Gnomologia, no. 5119 (1732).

421. Horses all stumble.

Chinese proverb

422. We shall take care not to vex the young horse, or cause it to abandon its affable gracefulness in disgust. For this is like the fragrance of blossoms, which never returns, once it has vanished.

Antoine de la Baume Pluvinel (ca. 1600)

423. Although the summer river has a bridge, Horses wade through the water.

Tsunenori Shiki (1867–1902)

424. And the horses which Solomon had were
brought out of Egypt.

I Kings 10:28

425. Their horses' hoofs shall be counted like flint.

Isaiah 5:28

426. With the hoofs of his horses
Shall he tread down all thy streets. . . .

Ezekiel 26:11

427. Sometimes he trots, as if he told the steps,
With gentle majesty and modest pride;
Anon he rears upright, curvets and leaps,
As who would say, lo! thus my strength is tried;
And this I do to capture the eye
Of the fair breeder that is standing by.

William Shakespeare (1564–1616),
Venus and Adonis (1592).

428. The horse is an archetypal symbol which
will always find ways to stir up deep and moving
ancestral memories in every human being.

Paul Mellon (1907–?), foreword to
Baskett, The Horse in Art (1980).

429. The difference between an author and a horse is that the horse doesn't understand the horse dealer's language.

Max Frisch (1911–?), in Unseld,
The Author and His Publisher (1980).

430. Said the little Eohippus,
    "I am going to be a horse,
    And on my middle finger-nails
    To run my earthly course!
    "I'm going to have a lowing tail!
    I'm going to have a mane!
    I'm going to stand fourteen hands high
    On the Psychozoic plain!"

Charlotte P. S. Gilman (1860–1935),
Similar Cases.

431. Bring forth the horses.

George Gordon, Lord Byron (1788–1824), *Mazeppa* (1819).

432. Steed threatens steed, in high and boastful neighs,
    Piercing the night's dull ear.

William Shakespeare (1564–1616),
Henry V, act 4, chorus (1598).

433. A full-hot horse; who being allowed his way,
Self-mettle tires him.

William Shakespeare (1564–1616),
Henry VIII, act 1, sc. 1 (1612).

434. The burden is equal to the horse's strength.

The Talmud

435. Horses have as much individuality and
character as people.

C. W. Anderson (1891–1971),
Complete Book of Horses and Horsemanship (1963).

436. Breed the best to the best and hope for the best.

breeder's axiom

437. St. George, thou saintly chevalier,
With all my heart I implore thee:
To mares and stallions thou are dear—
Secure one favor for me:
See here! My blood congeals with fright:
The pedigreed grand mare is foaling.
Give her the best of foals tonight,
And send my care a-rolling!

The horse breeder's prayer (traditional)

438. To God I speak Spanish, to women Italian, to men French, and to my horse—German.

Holy Roman Emperor Charles V (1500–1558)

439. Spanish is the language for lovers, Italian for singers, French for diplomats, German for horses, and English for geese.

Spanish proverb

440. What do we, as a nation, care about books? How much do you think we spend altogether on our libraries, public or private, as compared with what we spend on our horses?

John Ruskin (1819–1900), *Sesame and Lilies* (1865).

441. They sell the pasture to buy the horse.

William Shakespeare (1564–1616),
Henry V, pt. 2, act 1, chorus (1598).

442. Inventing a story with grass,
    I find a young horse
deep inside it.

James Dickey (1923–?),
A Birth (1962).

443. Men are generally more careful of the breed
of their horses and dogs than of their children.

William Penn (1644–1718),
Some Fruits of Solitude (1693).

444. And Ruksh, the horse,
  Who stood at hand, utter'd a dreadful cry:
  No horse's cry was that, most like the roar
  Of some pain'd desert lion, who all day
  Hath trailed the hunter's javelin in his side,
  And comes at night to die upon the sand.

Mathew Arnold (1822–1888),
Sohrab and Rustum (1853).

445. If he were a horse, nobody would buy him;
with that eye, no one could answer for his temper.

Walter Bagehot (1826–1877),
Biographical Studies, Essay 2, Lord Brougham (1881).

446. How the horse dominated the mind of the
early races, especially of the Mediterranean! You
were a lord if you had a horse. Far back, far back
in our dark soul the horse prances. . . . The horse,
the horse! The symbol of surging potency and
power of movement, of action, in man.

D. H. Lawrence (1885–1930), *Apocalypse* (1931).

447. Horses, a sort of animals which, as they dirty no sheets, are thought in inns to pay better for their beds than their riders, and are therefore considered as the more desirable company.

Henry Fielding (1707–1754), Tom Jones (1749).

448. Never thank yourself, always thank the horses for the happiness and joy we experience through them.

Hans H.-E. Isenbart,
in Isenbart and Bührer,
The Kingdom of the Horse (1969).

449. England is the paradise of women, the purgatory of men, and the hell of horses.

John Florio (1553–1625), Second Fruites (1591).

450. England is a paradise for women, and hell for horses; Italy a paradise for horses, hell for women, as the diverb goes.

Robert Burton (1577–1640),
Anatomy of Melancholy, sec. 3 (1621).

451. It is better to be a horse than a cart.

American proverb

452. If you have no horse, you walk, of course.

Yiddish proverb

453. Now the great winds shoreward blow,
Now the salt tides seaward flow;
Now the wild white horses play,
Champ and chafe and toss in the spray.

Mathew Arnold (1822–1888),
The Forsaken Merman (1849).

454. I know two things about the horse,
And one of them is rather coarse.

unknown, *The Week-End Book*.

455. A groaning horse and a groaning wife, never
fail their master.

John Heywood (1497–1580), *Proverbs* (1564).

456. The horse one cannot have always has a fault.

Danish proverb

457. [The horse is] the noblest conquest man has
ever made.

Georges de Buffon (1707–1788),
"Le Cheval," in *L'Histoiredes Mammiféres* (1775–1776).

458. Unhappy the horse whose rider is blind: it will never grow sleek.

Baltasar Gracián (1601–1658),
Oráculo Manual, Maxim 230 (1647).

459. Do not buy a horse with your eyes, but with your ears.

Czech proverb

460. They love their horses next to their kin.

J.R.R. Tolkien (1892–1973),
The Lord of the Rings, pt. 1,
The Fellowship of the Ring, rev. ed. (1965).

461. Like the horse to the meadow.

Plato (427–347 B.C.E.),
Theaetetus (ca. 369 B.C.E.).

462. Whose only fit companion is his horse.

William Cowper (1731–1800),
Conversation (1781).

463. Show me your horse and I will tell you what you are.

old English saying

464. The hooves of the horse! Oh! witching and sweet is the music earth steals from the iron-shod feet; no whisper of love, no trilling of bird, can stir me as hooves of the horse have stirred.

Will H. Ogilvie

465. Run slowly, horses of the night.

Ovid (43 B.C.E.–18 C.E.),
Amores, 13 (1 B.C.E.).

466. He doth nothing but talk of his horse.

William Shakespeare (1564–1616),
The Merchant of Venice, act 1, sc. 2 (1597).

467. The neck of the animal, before arched, as if in compassion . . . was now extended, at full length. . . . The eyes, before invisible, now wore an energetic and human expression, while they gleamed with a fiery and unusual red; and the  distended lips of the apparently enraged horse left in full view his sepulchral and disgusting teeth.

Edgar Allan Poe (1809–1849),
"Metzengerstein" (1831).

468. The nature of the horse remains unchanged, whether it carries the saddle of the prince, or whether it draws the cart of the wagoner. The noble ones accept the yoke, they serve, but will never be slaves, for to themselves they can never be traitors.

H.-H. Isenbart (1923–?),
in Isenbart and Bührer,
The Kingdom of the Horse (1969).

469. What is a horse but a species of four-footed dumb man, in a leathern overall, who happens to live upon oats, and toils for his masters, half-requited or abused, like the biped hewers of wood and drawers of water?

Herman Melville (1819–1891),
Redburn (1849).

470. Before the gods that made the gods
   Had seen their sunrise pass,
   The White Horse of the White Horse Vale
   Was cut out of the grass.

G. K. Chesterton (1874–1936),
Ballad of the White Horse, 1.

471. The King of France's horses are better housed than I.

Ernst August, Elector of Hanover (1629–1698)
[commenting on Louis XIV's stables at Versailles]

472. A lame cat is better than a swift horse when rats infest the stable.

Chinese proverb

473. My horses understand me tolerably well; I converse with them at least four hours every day. They are strangers to bridle or saddle; the live in great amity with me, and friendship to each other.

Jonathan Swift (1667–1745),
Gulliver's Travels,
Voyage to the Houyhnhnms, 2 (1725).

474. No foot, no horse.

anon.

475. A fly, sir, may sting a stately horse, and make him wince; but one is but an insect, and the other a horse still.

Samuel Johnson (1709–1784),
in Boswell, *Life of Johnson* (1763).

476. Beware of him as has no use for horses.

Winston Churchill (1871–1947), *Richard Carvel*, 4 (1899).

477. Dogs, like horses, are quadrupeds. That is to say, they have four rupeds, one at each corner, on which they walk.

Frank Muir (1920–?), in Muir and Norden,
You Can't Have Your Kayak and Heat It (1973).

478. And here I say to parents, especially wealthy parents, don't give your son money. As far as you can afford it, give him horses.

Winston Churchill (1874–1965),
My Early Life, ch. 4 (1930).

479. To confess that you are totally ignorant about the Horse, is social suicide: you will be despised by everybody, especially the horse.

W. C. Sellar and R. J. Yeatman, *Horse Nonsense*.

480. You may have my husband, but not my horse. My husband won't need emasculating, and my horse I won't have you meddle with. I'll preserve one last male thing in the museum of this world, if I can.

D.H. Lawrence (1885–1930), *Kangaroo* (1923).

481. The horse . . . has his head ever in the manger;... and a hungry dog eats dirty puddings.

Thomas Dekker (1570–1632), *The Pleasant Comedie of Old Fortunatus*, act 2, sc. 2 (1600).

482. Like the dog in the manger that neither ate the barley herself not permitted the hungry horse to eat it.

Lucian, *Timon*, ch. 14 (ca. 170).

483. Like unto cruel Dogges liying in a Maunger, neither eatiyng the Haye theim seelves ne sufferyng the Horse to feed there of hymself.

William Bullein (d. 1576), *A Dialogue Against the Fever-Pestilence* (1564).

484. Thou dealest with most of thy acquaintances as the Dogge doth in the maunger, who neither sufferesth the horse to eat hay, nor will himselfe.

John Lyly (1554–1606), *Euphues* (1579).

485. Like a Dog in the Manger; you'll not eat your selfe, nor let the Horse eat.

Thomas Fuller (1654–1734), *Gnomologia* no. 3322 (1732).

486. Many Dogs soon eat up a Horse.

Thomas Fuller (1654–1734), *Gnomologia* no. 3343 (1732).

487. The man who is born in a stable is a horse.

proverb

488. A man does sometimes become a horse by being born in a stable.

Michael Scott (1789–1835), *Tom Cringle's Log* (1833).

489. Being born in a stable does not necessarily make you a horse.

J. O'Faolain (1932–), *No Country for Young Men* (1980).

490. Even a good horse cannot keep running always.

Irish proverb

491. Lend not horse, nor wife, nor sword.

English proverb

492. Three things I never lends—my 'oss, my wife, and my name.

Robert Smith Surtees (1803–1864),
Hillingdon Hall, ch. 33 (1845)

493. Praise a horse after a month and a woman after a year.

Czech proverb

494. It is a good horse that has no faults.

French proverb

495. Two horses are not tied to one stake.

Turkish proverb

496. He has eaten a horse and the tail hangs out his mouth.

English proverb

497. He has taken my horse and left me the tether.

English proverb

498. All I say is, nobody has any business to go around looking like a horse and behaving as if it were all right. You don't catch horses going around looking like people, do you?

Dorothy Parker (1893–1967), *Horsie*.

499. It is the nature of the horse not to sleep but to nap.

The Talmud

500. A man is forbidden to sleep in the daytime longer than the sleep of a horse, which is equivalent to sixty respirations.

Succah 26b

501. Goodness! It would be cheaper to buy a horse and just be kind to it!

> Woman commenting on the
> ticket price for an ASPCA theatre
> benefit, in Uris, *Say it Again* (1979).

502. Most people who decide to buy a horse suffer from one delusion or another.

There are cowboy delusions, Black Beauty delusions and . . . the Tom Jones delusion, which is inevitably tied to notions of gentility, wealth, and foxes.

> Christopher Dickey, "The Horsey Look:
> Riddling Wallets to Corral Dreams,"
> *The Washington Post*, October 14, 1976, sec. D.

503. Pony people don't horse around.

> printed on a T-shirt (1989)

504. A pony comes out of a gourd.

> Japanese proverb

505. Happiness is never outgrowing your favorite pony.

> seen on a sweatshirt (1991)

Part Two

Donkeys & Mules

506. If I know'd a donkey
wot wouldn't go
   To see Mrs. Jarley's
waxwork show,
   do you think I'd
acknowledge him,
      Oh no no!

Charles Dickens (1812–1870),
The Old Curiosity Shop (1840–1841).

507. The man who argues with the braying of the
donkey or the barking of his dog will win no
cases before the high courts.

Marion Zimmer Bradley (1930–),
Thendara House (1983).

508. He is an ass that brays against an ass.

English proverb

509. If a donkey brays at you, don't bray at him.

George Herbert (1593–1633),
Jacula Prudentum (1640).

510. Because a Donkey takes a whim
To Bray at You, why Bray at Him?

Arthur Guiterman (1871–1943),
A Poet's Proverbs (1924).

511. Every time donkey bray, him remember
something.

Jamaican proverb

512. It is better to be mute than with an ass
to dispute.

English proverb

513. If a house could be built by a loud voice,
an ass would build two in a day.

Apocrypha: Ahikar, 2.8 (50 B.C.E.)

514. A donkey likes its snort as a canary its song.

Joseph Caspi (1297–1340),
commentary to Proverbs 23:15

515. A donkey may be schooled for a hundred
years, and only learn to bray louder.

Marion Zimmer Bradley (1930–),
Thendara House (1983).

516. The ass that brays most eats least.

English proverb

517. About a donkey's taste why need we fret us?
To lips like his a thistle is a lettuce.

William Ewart (1798–1869)

518. A thistle is a fat salad for an ass's mouth.

English proverb

519. A donkey must not die before his grass grows.

Serbian proverb

520. If you find them worshiping a donkey, bring him grass.

Moorish proverb

521. Since when is there a donkey who does not like green grass?

Mexican-American proverb

522. Until the Donkey tried to clear
The Fence, he thought himself a deer.

Arthur Guiterman (1871–1943),
A Poet's Proverbs (1924).

523. Perhaps your mimic roar may deceive strangers, but to me you will always be a donkey.

Avianus, *Fables* (ca. 400).

524. The donkey-drivers think one thing and the donkeys think another.

Montaiglon, "La Borgoise d'orliens,"
in *Recueil des Fabliaux* (ca. 1250).

525. One poor ass cannot carry two burdens.

English proverb

526. Better a sound donkey than a comsumptive philosopher.

Romanian proverb

527. Donkey tied, master tranquil.

Greek proverb

528. Tie the ass where the owner wants.

Arabic proverb

529. An ass must be tied where his master will have him.

English proverb

530. I shall not tie the donkey in the place of the horse (said the widow of a high-born man in refusing the marriage proposal of a low-born man).

Moorish proverb

531. He who took the donkey up to the roof should bring it down.

Lebanese proverb

532. He who takes a donkey up a minaret must bring it down.

Arabic proverb

533. The man who brings a gift on a donkey will receive one on a camel.

Arabic proverb

534. Only a donkey is patient under a load.

African (Hausa) proverb

535. The donkey knows seven ways to swim; when he falls into the water, he forgets them all.

Armenian proverb

536. To the donkey the sea is only knee-deep.

Serbian proverb

537. The small donkey is the one everybody rides.

Libyan proverb

538. When the donkey wants to spite his master, he dies.

Armenian proverb

539. You can recognize a donkey by his long ears, a fool by his long tongue.

Yiddish proverb

540. The veriest Asses hide their ears most.

English proverb

541. He who owns the donkey holds him by the tail.

German proverb

542. The donkey doesn't know his tail until he has lost it.

Haitian proverb

543. The rented donkey always dies.

Arabic proverb

544. Other people's donkey best turns the mill.

Chinese proverb

545. You'll get no laurel crown for outrunning a burro.

Martial [Marcus Valerius Martialis] (40–100)

546. As great a waste of effort, as to train an ass
To race upon the campus, obedient to the reins.

Horace (65–8 B.C.E.),
Satires, bk. 1, sat. 1 (35 B.C.E.).

547. Donkey gallop soon over.

proverb

548. You can take an old mule and run him and
feed him and train him and get him in the best
shape of his life, but you ain't going to win the
Kentucky Derby!

Pepper Martin (1904–1965),
in Broun, *Tumultuous Merriment* (1979).

549. There's no need to goad a moving donkey.

Arabic proverb

550. An ass laden with gold can enter the gates of any city.

Philip of Macedon (382–366 B.C.E.)

551. An ass loaded with gold goes lightly up a mountain.

Miguel de Cervantes Saavedra (1547–1616),
Don Quixote de la Mancha, pt. 2 (1605–1616).

552. There's no fence or fortress against an ass laden with gold.

James Howell (1594–1666),
Familiar Letters (1645–1655).

553. There is not any place so high whereunto an ass laden with gold will not get up.

James Mabbe (1572–1642),
Celestina (1631).

554. As ass is but an ass, though laden with gold.

Thomas Fuller (1654–1734),
Gnomologia, no. 585 (1732).

555. An ass is an ass, even when it carries the sultan's treasure.

Lebanese proverb

556. Smile at him and he brings his donkey in as well.

Lebanese proverb

557. Doth the wild ass bray when he hath grass?

Job 6:5

558. A hungry ass heeds not a blow.

Erasmus (1466–1536),
Adagia, ch. 2 (1523).

559. Hay is more acceptable to an ass than gold.

Latin proverb

560. The ass loaded with gold still eats thistles.

German proverb

561. Honey is not for the ass's mouth.

Miguel de Cervantes Saavedra (1547–1616),
Don Quixote de la Mancha, pt. 1 (1605–1616).

562. Give an ass oats and he runs after thistles.

George Herbert (1593–1633),
Jacula Prudentum (1640).

563. The ass often carries gold on his back, yet feeds on thistles.

James Howell (1594–1666),
Parly of Beasts (1660).

564. The ass that carrieth wine drinketh water.

Thomas Fuller (1654–1734),
Gnomologia (1732).

565. An ass is beautiful to an ass, and a pig to a pig.

John Ray (1627–1705),
English Proverbs (1670).

566. To shear the ass.

proverb [meaning something impossible to do]

567. One burro scratches the other.

Mexican-American proverb

568. Who washes an ass's head loseth both labor and soap.

John Florio (1553–1625), *First Fruites* (1578).

569. What does a donkey know about ginger?

Moroccan proverb

570. When a donkey is well off he goes dancing on ice.

Czech proverb

571. The law is an ass—an idiot.

Charles Dickens (1812–1870),
Oliver Twist (1838).

572. I am ashamed the law is such an ass.

George Chapman (1559–1634),
Revenge for Honour (1634).

573. I had rather ride on an ass that carries me than a horse that throws me.

George Herbert (1593–1633),
Jacula Prudentum (1640).

574. Better an ass that carries us than a horse that throws us.

J. G. Holland (1819–1881),
Gold-Foil the Infallible (1895).

575. The ass thinks one thing, and he that rides him another.

Thomas D'Urfey (1653–1723),
Quixote, pt. 3, act 3, sc. 2 (1694–1696).

576. Better strive with an ill ass than carry the wood one's self.

Thomas Fuller (1653–1734),
Gnomologia, no. 930 (1732).

577. A sharp goad for a stubborn ass.

French proverb

578. A dull ass near home needs no spur.

Thomas Fuller (1654–1734),
Gnomologia, no. 83 (1732).

579. Your dull ass will not mend his pace with beating.

William Shakespeare (1564–1616),
Hamlet, act 5, sc. 1 (1600).

580. There's no need to goad a moving donkey.

Arabic proverb

581. The pace of an ass depends on his barley.

The Talmud

582. True, the poor ass is dull; but then for carrying loads, 'tis dear to men.

Saadi [Sheikh Muslih Addin] (1184–1292),
Gulistan, ch. 1 (1258).

583. The ass will carry his load but not a double load; ride not a free horse to death.

Miguel de Cervantes Saavedra (1547–1616),
Don Quixote de la Mancha, pt. 4 (1605–1616).

584. Other folks burden kills the ass.

Miguel de Cervantes Saavedra (1547–1616),
Don Quixote de la Mancha, pt. 2 (1605–1616).

585. Asses are made to bear, and so are you.

William Shakespeare (1564–1616),
The Taming of the Shrew, act 2, sc. 1 (1593).

586. When I am coupled with you,
Unequal to the load that you can bear,
I the poor ass shall founder in the mire.

Titus Maccius Plautus (254–184 B.C.E.),
Aulularia, act 2, sc. 2.

587. A man who cannot beat his ass, beats the saddle.

Petronius (d. 66), Satryicon.

588. The fault of the ass must not be laid upon the pack-saddle.

Miguel de Cervantes Saavedra (1547–1616),
Don Quixote de la Mancha, pt. 2 (1605–1616).

589. An ass's load does not include the saddle.

Turkish proverb

590. Repetition teaches the donkey.

Saudi Arabian proverb

591. If I were a prince and you were a prince, who would drive the asses?

Maltese proverb

592. Things have come to a hell of a pass when a man can't wallop his own jackass.

anon., ca. 1900

593. He shall be buried with the burial of an ass.

Jeremiah 22:19

594. An empty man will get understanding when a wild ass's colt is born a man.

Job 11:12

595. If the ass is summoned to the wedding it is to carry wood.

Arabic proverb

596. He who drives an ass must of necessity smell its wind.

Arabic proverb

597. By outward show let's not be cheated;
An ass should like an ass be treated.

John Gay (1685–1732), Fables:
The Packhorse and the Carrier (1727).

598. The ass which puts on the lion's skin (thinking that thereby his master would more respect him) was known for an ass, and used like an ass.

Stefano Guazzo (1530–1593),
Civil Conversations (1574).

599. Clad in a lion's shaggy hide,
An ass spread terror far and wide.

> Jean La Fontaine (1621–1695),
> *Fables*: The Ass in the Lion's Skin (1665).

600. What good can it do an ass to be called
a lion?

> Thomas Fuller (1654–1734),
> *Gnomologia*, no. 5490 (1732)

601. When a jackass brays, no one pays any
attention to him, not even other jackasses. But
when a lion brays like a jackass, even the lions
in the neighborhood may be pardoned for
exhibiting a little surprise.

> G. J. Nathan (1882–1958),
> *Testament of a Critic* (1931).

602. Even when the ass wears the lion's skin, its
ears betray it.

> German version of Aesop's
> "Ass in the Lion's Skin"

603. For fear of the lion the ass left his burden.

> Ahikar, *Teachings*, col. 6, li. 89 (ca. 550 B.C.E.).

604. Lions led by donkeys.

attributed to Erich Ludendorff (1865–1937)

605. A live ass is more useful than a dead lion.

E. C. R. Lorac [Edith Caroline Rivett] (1894–1958),
The Affair at Thor's Head (1935).

606. A willing donkey was a better proposition than a reluctant lion.

Violet Powell (1912–?),
A Substantial Ghost (1967).

607. I'd rather be a live jackass than a dead lion.

Jack Vizzard (1914–), *See No Evil* (1970).

608. I'd sooner be a live donkey than a dead sitting duck any old day of the week.

Joyce Porter (1924–),
Dover Strikes Again (1973).

609. A live donkey is worth two dead heroes, any day.

L. Brock [Alister McAllister] (1877–?),
The Stoke Silver Case (1929).

610. An unlettered king is a crowned ass.

anon.

611. As lazy as a donkey.

Irish proverb

612. Like the ass's tail, it never grows longer or shorter.

Arabic proverb

613. An ass is cold even in the summer solstice.

John Ray (1627–1705),
Hebrew Proverbs (1678).

614. He that loves Glass without G,
Take away L and that is he.

John Ray (1627–1705),
English Proverbs (1670).

615. One ass calls another long-ears.

German proverb

616. The ass is known by his ears.

Latin proverb

617. Who is there that has not the ears of an ass?

Persius (34–62 C.E.), *Satires*, sat. 1.

618. Hood an ass with rev'rend purple,
So you can hide his two ambitious ears,
And he shall pass for a cathedral doctor.

Ben Jonson (1573–1637),
Volpone, act 1, sc. 1 (1605).

619. If one says you have the ears of an ass, pay no attention, but if two tell you that, get yourself a halter.

Jewish proverb

620. When you go to a donkey house don't talk about ears.

Jamaican proverb

621. I am an ass, indeed; you may prove it by my long ears.

William Shakespeare (1564–1616),
The Comedy of Errors, act 4, sc. 4 (1588–1593).

622. If thy comrade calls thee ass, put the saddle upon thy back.

Babylonian Talmud: Baba Kamma (ca. 450)

623. When everyone tells you you are an ass, thank God and pray.

Moorish proverb

624. He that makes himself an ass, must not take it ill if men ride him.

Thomas Fuller (1654–1734),
Gnomologia, no. 3232 (1732).

625. Why, what an ass am I!

William Shakespeare (1564–1616),
Hamlet, act 2, sc. 2 (1600).

626. We make ourselves asses, and then everybody will ride us.

C. H. Spurgeon (1834–1892),
John Ploughman, ch. 4 (1869)

627. 'Tis true; she rides me and I long for grass. 'Tis so, I am an ass.

William Shakespeare (1564–1616),
The Comedy of Errors, act 2, sc. 2 (1588–1593).

628. I've made an ass of myself so many times I often wonder if I am one.

Norman Mailer (1931–),
New York Times Magazine,
September 9, 1979.

629. You pride yourself upon an animal faculty in respect to which . . . the jackass [is] infinitely your superior.

John Randolph of Roanoake (1773–1833),
[in response to Tristram Burges' public taunt
on Randolph's sexual impotence] ca. 1820 .

630. I have been an author for twenty years and an ass for fifty-five.

Mark Twain (1835–1910), letter (1890)

631. By the wrongs I suffer, and the blows I bear.
　　I should kick, being kick'd; and being at
that pass,
　　You would keep from my heels and beware
of an ass.

William Shakespeare (1564–1616),
The Comedy of Errors, act 3, sc. 1 (1588–1593).

632. When all tell thee thou art an ass, 'tis time for thee to bray.

John Heywood (1497–1580), *Proverbs* (1564).

633. Every ass loves to hear himself bray.

Thomas Fuller (1654–1734),
Gnomologia, no. 1404 (1732);
also a Yiddish folk saying.

634. What has the ass to do with a lyre?

Lucian (ca. 120–180)

635. It is better to look like an ass than fight with one.

Francis Beeding [John Palmer (1885–1944) and
Hillary Aiden St. George Saunders (1898–1951)],
Heads off at Midnight (1938).

636. Jest with an ass, and he will flap you in the face with his tail.

H. G. Bohn (1796–1884),
Handbook of Proverbs (1855).

637. When you see an ass mount a ladder, you will find some sense in fools.

Jewish proverb

638. I've a shelter for the hens and a stable for the ass,

And what can a man want more?

Brian Friel (1929–), *Little Brigid Flynn*.

639. Every ass thinks himself worthy to stand with the king's horses.

John Clarke (1609–1676), *Paroemiologia* (1639).

640. He who is an ass and thinks himself a deer,
When he tries to leap the ditch, his error
will be clear.

Charles Cahier, *Six Mille Proverbs* (1856).

641. It's better to be killed by a robber than by
the kick of an ass.

Portuguese proverb

642. No wise man stands behind an ass when
he kicks.

Terence (190–159 B.C.E.), *The Eunuch* (161 B.C.E.).

643. The horse kicks out and the mule kicks out;
between the two the donkey dies.

Turkish proverb

644. Take heed of an ox before, an ass behind,
and a monk on all sides.

John Ray (1627–1705), *English Proverbs* (1678).

645. As straight as a donkey's
hind leg.

proverb

646. For donkey's years.

proverb [meaning a very long time]

647. One could drag a donkey to a well, but getting it to drink was another matter.

John Symonds, *Bezill* (1962).

648. Like a donkey between two bundles of hay.

proverb [meaning indecisiveness;
referring to the old tale of the donkey
that starved because he couldn't decide
which bale of hay to eat first]

649. A narrow lane, and the ass is kicking.

John Lewis Burkhardt (1784–1817),
Arabic Proverbs, no. 315 (1817).

650. If an ass goes a travelling, he'll not come home a horse.

Thomas Fuller (1654–1734),
Gnomologia (1732).

651. He that does a serious business in haste rides post upon an ass.

James Howell (1594–1666),
New Sayings (1659).

652. There are three without rule: a mule, a pig and a woman.

Irish (Donegal) proverb

653. As stubborn as Carter's mule.

proverb

654. As stubborn as a mule.

proverb

655. I am the mule—the butt of countless jokes. . . .

Will Chamberlain

656. A mule has neither pride of ancestry nor hope of posterity.

Robert Green Ingersoll (1833–1899)

657. The mule is haf hoss and haf jackass, and then kums a full stop, natur discovering her mistake.

Josh Billings [Henry Wheeler Shaw]
(1818–1885), On Mules.

658. The Almighty permitted man to create two things after Creation. One was fire . . . the other was the mule, which was produced by cross-breeding.

Pesachim 54a

659. Only a mule denies his origin.

Arabic proverb

660. Mules make a great fuss about their ancestors having been horses.

German proverb

661. No statues are raised to mules.

Guy Owen (1925–), "Poem to a Mule,
Dead Twenty Years," in
Cole, *Poems One Line and Longer* (1973).

662. The mule is an aristocrat, one of the last classical allusions in this illiterate world.

Coleman Barks, *The Mule* (1972).

663. In my mind those which extol themselves in words and brag of their birth, rather disgrace themselves than otherwise . . . Like the mule who being demanded of his birth, and being ashamed to say he was an ass's son, answered, that he was a horse's cousin.

Stefano Guazzo (1530–1593),
Civil Conversations (1574).

664. The mule goes slowly, but goes day and night.

Saadi [Sheikh Muslih Addin] (1184–1292),
Gulistan, ch. 6 (1258).

665. When mules foal.

Herodotus (5th century B.C.E.), *History* (ca. 455 B.C.E.)
[meaning something that will never happen].

666. He fattens the mule and starves the horse.

William Scarborough, *Chinese Proverbs*, no. 600.

667. The mule always keeps a kick in reserve for its master.

French proverb

668. He who looks for a mule without fault must go on foot.

Spanish proverb

Part Three
Horsemanship, Work and Sport

669. A horse! A horse! My kingdom for a horse!

> William Shakespeare (1564–1616),
> *Richard III*, act 5, sc. 4 (1592).

670. For want of a nail the shoe is lost,
For want of a shoe the horse is lost,
For want of a horse the rider is lost.

> George Herbert (1593–1633),
> *Jacula Prudentum* (1640).

671. A little neglect may breed mischief:
For want of a nail the shoe was lost,
For want of a shoe the horse was lost,
For want of a horse the rider was lost,
For want of a rider the battle was lost,
For want of a battle a kingdom was lost—
and all for the want of a horseshoe nail.

> Benjamin Franklin (1706–1790),
> *Poor Richard's Almanack* (1757).

672. A nail may save the horseshoe, the horseshoe may save the horse, the horse may save the rider, and the rider may save the kingdom.

> Turkish proverb

673. When a man rides his horse he forgets about God, and when he dismounts he forgets about his horse.

Arabic proverb

674. Behold, he cometh up as clouds,
    And his chariots are as the whirlwind;
    His horses are swifter than eagles—
    Woe unto us. We are undone.

Jeremiah 4:13

675. And with thee will I shatter the horse and his rider,
    And with thee will I shatter the chariot and him that rideth therein. . . .

Jeremiah 51:21

676. Hark! the whip and hark! the rattling of wheels,
    And prancing horses and bounding chariots;
    The horsemen charging, And the flashing sword. . . .

Nahum 3:2–3

677. To horse, away!

William Shakespeare (1564–1616),
Richard III, act 5, sc. 3 (1592).

678. How many knights be there now in England
that have the use and the exercise of a knight?
That is, to wit, that he knows his horse and his
horse knows him.

William Caxton (1422–1491),
The Order of Chivalry (1484).

679. After God, we owed our victory to our
horses.

Don Pedro de Casteneda de Nagera (ca. 1560)
[a conquistador writing of the Spanish
victory over the native peoples of the Americas]

680. Villain, a horse—
Villain, I say, give me a horse to fly,
To swim the river, villain, and to fly.

George Peele (1558–1597),
Battle of Alcazar, act 5 (1594).

681. If there's a horse you can always find a whip.

Yiddish folk saying

682. One whip is enough for a good horse, for a bad one not a thousand.

Russian proverb

683. You whip your poor horse too much. He gallops so much that he's exhausted, yet he never leaves the stable.

"Cho-Je" [played by Kevin Lindsay] in
"Planet of the Spiders" episode (1974)
of the television series Doctor Who;
screenplay by Robert Sloman.

684. I wish your horses swift and sure of foot;
And so I do command you to their backs.

William Shakespeare (1564–1616),
Macbeth, act 3, sc. 1 (1605).

685. The horse is the strength of the army. The horse is a moving bulwark.

unknown, The Hitopadeṣa, 3 (ca. 500).

686. A young trooper should have an old horse.

H. G. Bohn, Handbook of Proverbs (1855).

687. A horseman unarmed is like a bird without wings.

Moroccan proverb

688. A scabbed horse is good enough for a scabbed knight.

Thomas Fuller (1654–1732),
Gnomologia, no. 385 (1732).

689. The horse is prepared against the day of battle;
But the victory is of the Lord.

Proverbs 21:31

690. Cavalry horses delight in battle.

Chinese proverb

691. The man on horseback knows nothing of the toil of the traveler on foot.

Chinese proverb

692. Depend upon thyself and thy horse.

Montenegrin proverb

693. The courser paw'd the ground with restless feet,
And snorting, foam'd, and champ'd the golden bit.

John Dryden (1631–1700)

694. Lincoln was asked what he would reply to McClellan's earlier advice on how to carry on the affairs of the nation. And Lincoln answered, "Nothing—but it made me think of the story of the man whose horse kicked up and stuck his foot through the stirrup. He said to the horse, 'If you are going to get on I will get off.'"

Carl Sandburg (1878–1967),
*Abraham Lincoln: The Prairie Years
and the War Years* (1954).

695. What though thyn hors be bothe foule and lene,
If he wol serve thee rekke nat a bene.

Geoffrey Chaucer (1340–1400), prologue to
"The Nun's Priest's Tale," *The Canterbury Tales* (1387).

696. Be blithe, although you ride upon a jade.
What though your horse may be both foul and lean,
If he but serves you, don't care a bean.

J. U. Nicolson, *Canterbury Tales
in Modern English* (1934).

697. Know a horse riding him, a person associating with him.

Japanese proverb

698. While one never forgets entirely how to ride, it is easy to forget how big horses are, what little regard they have for the frailty of human flesh and how incredibly, well, beastly they are.

Christopher Dickey, "The Horsey Look:
Riddling Wallets to Corral Dreams" in
The Washington Post, October 14, 1976, sec. D.

699. Rodeoing is about the only sport you can't fix. You'd have to talk to the bulls and horses, and they wouldn't understand you.

Bill Linderman (1922–1961), March 1954

700. A woman never looks better than on horseback.

Jane Austen (1775–1817), *The Watsons* (1871).

701. People on horses look better than they are. People in cars look worse than they are.

Myra Mannes (1904–1990), *More in Anger* (1958).

702. The ship is the horse of the sea.

George Bernard Shaw (1856–1950),
Heartbreak House, act 3 (1913).

703. He may as well go on foot, they say, who
leads his horse by the bridle.

Michel de Montaigne (1533–1592),
Essays, bk. 3 (1595).

704. It is good walking with a horse in one's hand.

George Herbert (1593–1633),
Jacula Prudentum (1640).

705. Beggars mounted run their horse to death.

William Shakespeare (1564–1616),
Henry VI, pt. 3, act 1, sc. 4 (1591).

706. Even the beggars ride on horses.

Juan Garay (1527–1583)

707. Set a beggar on horseback, and he will gallop.

William Camden (1551–1623),
Remains Concerning Britain (1605).

708. If wishes were
horses, beggars
would ride.

John Ray (1607–1725),
English Proverbs (1670).

709. Set a beggar on horseback and he will ride a gallop.

Robert Burton (1577–1640),
The Anatomy of Melancholy, pt. 2 (1621).

710. Set a beggar on horseback and he'll outride the Devil.

German proverb

711. Put a beggar on horseback and he'll ride to hell.

Irish proverb

712. Put a beggar on horseback and he'll go a gallop.

Irish proverb

713. Spur not an unbroken horse.

Sir Walter Scott (1771–1832),
The Monastery (1820).

714. Spur a free horse, he'll run himself to death.

Ben Jonson (1573–1637),
Tale of a Tub (1633).

715. A good horse should be seldom spurred.

Thomas Fuller (1654–1734),
Gnomologia, no. 166 (1732).

716. A good horse oft needs a good spur.

John Clarke (1609–1676),
Paroemiologia Anglo-Latina (1639).

717. It is the bridle and spur that makes a good horse.

Thomas Fuller (1654–1734),
Gnomologia, no. 3021 (1732).

718. You have set spurs to a willing horse.

Pliny the Younger (Gaius Plinius Caecillus Secundus)
(62–113 C.E.), *Epistles*, bk. i, epistle 8.

719. Another man's horse and your own spurs outrun the wind.

German proverb

720. But hollow men, like horses hot at hand,
   Make gallant show and promise of their mettle;
   But when they should endure the bloody spur,
   They fall their crests, and, like deceitful jades,
   Sink in the trial.

William Shakespeare (1564–1616),
Julius Caesar, act 4, sc. 2 (1599).

721. Here, when they heard the horse-bells ring,
The ancient Britons dressed and rode
To watch the dark Phoenicians bring
Their goods along the Western Road.

Rudyard Kipling (1865–1936),
"Merrow Downs, in *Just So Stories* (1902).

722. Better ride a good horse for a year than an
ass all your life.

Dutch proverb

723. It's the willing horse they saddle the most.

Jamaican proverb

724. How fondly dost thou spur a forward horse.

William Shakespeare (1564–1616),
Richard II, act 4, sc. 1 (1595).

725. By too much spurring the horse is made dull.

Stefano Guazzo (1530–1593),
Civil Conversations (1574).

726. For a big horse, wear big spurs.

Mexican-American proverb

727. A fast horse does not want the spur.

Portuguese proverb

728. Take a horse by his bridle and a man by his word.

Dutch proverb

729. An orator without judgement is a horse without a bridle.

Theophrastus (372–287 B.C.E.)

730. A man can no more make a safe use of wealth without reason, than he can of a horse without a bridle.

Socrates (470–399 B.C.E.)

731. The ear of a bridled horse is in his mouth.

Horace (65–8 B.C.E.), *Epistles*, bk. 1 (20 B.C.E.).

732. To bridle the horse by the tail.

French proverb
[meaning to start at the wrong end]

733. A horse is petted just before it is bridled.

Slovakian proverb

734. A golden bit does not make the horse any better.

French and Italian proverb

735. A gilded bit does not make a bad horse a good one.

Seneca (4 B.C.E.–65 C.E.),
Epistolae XLI, 6 (63–65 C.E.).

736. A hard bit does not make the better horse.

Danish proverb

737. It is not the gilt bridle that maketh the horse the better.

Stefano Guazzo (1530–1593),
Civil Conversations (1574).

738. The goodness of a horse goes in at his mouth.

G. J. Whyte-Melville (1821–1889), *Inside the Bar* (1861).

739. Boot, saddle, to horse and away!

Robert Browning (1812–1889),
Cavalier Tunes, Boot and Saddle Refrain (1842).

740. Things are in the saddle,
And ride mankind.

Ralph Waldo Emerson (1803–1882),
Poems: Ode, Inscribed to W. H. Channing (1847).

741. Saddle White Surrey for the field tomorrow.

William Shakespeare (1564–1616),
Richard III, act 8 (1592).

742. I will win the horse or lose the saddle.

proverb

743. To win the mare or lose the halter.

proverb

744. This same philosophy is a good horse in the stable, but an arrant jade on a journey.

Oliver Goldsmith (1728–1784),
The Good-Natured Man, act 1 (1768).

745. O happy horse, to bear the weight of Antony!

William Shakespeare (1564–1616),
Antony and Cleopatra, act 1, sc. 5 (1606).

746. I had a little pony,
His name was Dapple Grey;
I lent him to a lady,
To ride a mile away.
She whipped him, she slashed him,
She rode him through the mire;
I would not lend my pony now
For all the lady's hire.

unknown, *I Had a Little Pony*

747. The English country gentleman galloping after a fox—the unspeakable in full pursuit of the uneatable.

Oscar Wilde (1854–1900),
A Woman of No Importance (1893).

748. To ride to hounds is very glorious; but to have ridden to hounds is more glorious still.

Anthony Trollope (1815–1882),
Phineas Finn (1869).

749. Some horses are so polite that when they come to a fence, they stop and let you go over first.

anon.

750. There is something about jumping a horse over a fence, something that makes you feel good. Perhaps it's the risk, the gamble. In any event it's a thing I need.

William Faulkner (1897–1962),
in *The National Observer*, February 3, 1964.

751. The strongest horse loups the dyke.

James Kelly, *Scottish Proverbs* (1721).

752. Let the best horse leap the hedge first.

Thomas Fuller (1654–1734), *Gnomologia* (1732).

753. . . . it was all so ponderously weighted that when the big hurdles approached, the horse couldn't jump.

Kenneth Tynan (1927–1980),
review of Sybil Thorndike in *Oedipus Rex*,
in Rigg, *No Turn Unstoned* (1983)

754. Ride a horse and a mare toward the shoulders, an ass and a mule towards the buttocks.

James Howell (1594–1666),
Proverbs: English-Italian (1659).

755. An two men ride of a horse, one must ride behind.

William Shakespeare (1564–1616),
Much Ado About Nothing, act 3, sc. 5 (1598).

756. You ride so near the rump, you'll let none get on behind you. You will let none get any advantage by you.

James Kelly, *Scottish Proverbs* (1721).

757. Either I am the fore horse in the team, or I am none.

John Fletcher (1579–1625),
The Two Noble Kinsmen, act 1, sc. 2 (1613).

758. He that rides behind another, must not think to guide.

Thomas Fuller (1654–1734),
Gnomologia, no. 2270 (1732).

759. The biggest horses are not the best travellers.

Thomas Fuller (1654–1734),
Gnomologia, no. 4435 (1732).

760. The sight of a horse makes the traveller lame.

Indian (Bengali) proverb

761. A flea-bitten horse never tires.

proverb

762. The flea-bitten horse proveth always good in travel.

Barnaby Googe (1540–1594),
Four Books of Husbandry, 2 (1577).

763. I must not hang all my bells upon one horse.

James Howell (1594–1666),
English Proverbs (1659) .

764. The horse knows his rider, and a wife her husband.

Indian (Tamil) proverb

765. Seek for a good rider under his horse's feet.

Welsh proverb

766. God forgive you for galloping when trotting's not a sin.

Scottish proverb

767. A horned snake in the path,
That biteth the horse's heels,
so that his rider falleth backward.

Genesis 49:17

768. He rideth well that never fell.

Sir Thomas Malory (fl. ca. 1470),
Le Morte D'Arthur (1485).

769. He rides firm that fell never.

David Ferguson, Scottish Proverbs (1595).

770. It is not enough for a man to know how to ride, he must know how to fall.

anon.

771. Once mounted on the horse one must be able to withstand his eventual starts and bolts.

Mexican proverb

772. He's a gentle horse that never cast his rider.

James Kelly, *Scottish Proverbs* (1721).

773. Amidst his most swift and easy pace the rider must guard himself against a fall. . . .

Sir Walter Scott (1771–1832),
The Talisman (1825).

774. No one ever notices how you ride till you fall off.

Cooky McClung, "The Rules of the Day,"
The Chronicle of the Horse, October 7, 1983.

775. O thou, my milk-white pony, whose coat is as the moon-beams of this autumn night, carry me like a bird through the air. . . .

Murasaki Shikabu (974–1031),
The Tale of Genji, vol. 2,
The Sacred Tree, ch. 1 (1001–1015).

776. A good horseman is a man on the ground.

Irish proverb

777. A halterless horse is not mounted.

Turkish proverb

778. A hired horse tires never.

English proverb

779. He needs must trot afoot that tires his horse.

Thomas Heywood (1572–1641),
A Woman Killed with Kindness, act 4, sc. 6 (1607).

780. Better a lame horse than go afoot.

German proverb

781. Half the failures in life arise from pulling in one's horse as he is leaping.

Julius Hare (1795–1885) and
Augustus Hare (1792–1834), *Guesses at Truth*, 1.

782. It is not best to swap horses while crossing the river.

Abraham Lincoln (1809–1865), reply (June 9, 1864)
to a delegation from the National Union League.

783. Change horses in midstream if you want.

Hugh Pentecost [Judson Pentecost Philips] (1903–?),
The Twenty-Fourth Horse (1940).

784. A canter is the cure for every evil.

Benjamin Disraeli (1804–1881), *The Young Duke* (1831).

785. No hour of life is lost that is spent in the saddle.

Winston Churchill (1874–1965)

786. A good horse never lacks a saddle.

Italian proverb

787. The great advantage of a dialogue on horseback: it can be merged at any minute into a trot or canter, and one might escape from Socrates himself in the saddle.

George Eliot (1819–1880), *Adam Bede* (1859).

788. The best cure in the world for writer's block is a canter through the woods.

Cooky McClung, "First Things First,"
The Chronicle of the Horse, October 7, 1988.

789. Tis the abilities of the horse that occasion his slavery.

Thomas Fuller (1654–1734),
Gnomologia, no. 5117 (1732.)

790. If a man has lost his way in a dark winter's night, let him leave the horse to himself and the horse will find the way.

> William Cavendish, Marquis of Newcastle (1592–1676),
> *New Method of Dressing Horses* (1743).

791. More belongs to riding than a pair of boots.

> German proverb

792. Then hey, for boot and horse, lad,
And round the world away.

> Charles Kingsley (1819–1875),
> *The Water-Babies* (1863).

793. Sing, riding's a joy! For me I ride.

> Robert Browning (1812–1889),
> *The Last Ride Together*, st. 7 (1855).

794. All in green went my love riding
on a great horse of gold
into the silver dawn.

> e.e. cummings (1894–1962),
> *All In Green Went My Love Riding* (1923).

795. When you ride a young colt, see your saddle be well girt.

> English proverb

796. He that is manned with boys and horsed with colts shall have his meat eaten and his work undone.

English proverb

797. If you look at the ground, you'll end up on the ground.

unknown [advice on riding over jumps]

798. Head up, heels down.

anon.

799. Nothing is new in equitation, we only learn to see more.

anon.

800. In time the horses are taught to endure the restraining bit.

Ovid (43 B.C.E.–18 C.E.), Ars Amatoria, bk. 1 (1 B.C.E.).

801. Those that tame wild horses
  Pace 'em not in their hands to make 'em gentle,
  But stop their mouths with stubborn bits, an
spur 'em,
  Till they obey the manage.

William Shakespeare (1564–1616),
Henry VIII, act 5, sc. 3 (1612).

802. The trainer trains the docile horse to turn, with his sensitive neck, whichever way the rider indicates.

Horace (65–8 B.C.E.), *Epistles*, bk. 1 (20 B.C.E.).

803. If anybody expects to calm a horse down by tiring him out with riding swiftly and far, his supposition is just the reverse of the truth.

Xenophon (430–355 B.C.E.)

804. . . . Roan Barbary,
    That horse that thou so often hast bestrid,
    That horse that I so carefully have dres'd.
    That jade hath eat bread from my royal hand;
    This hand hath made him proud with
clapping him.
    Would he not stumble? would he not fall down,
    Since pride must have a fall, and break the neck
    Of that proud man that did usurp his back?
    Forgiveness, horse! why do I rail on thee,
    Since thou, created to be awed by man,
    Wast born to bear? I was not made a horse;
    And yet I bear a burthen like an ass,
    Spur-gall'd and tired by jauncing Bolingbroke.

William Shakespeare (1564–1616),
Richard II, act 5, sc. 5 (1595).

805. If one induces the horse to assume that carriage which it would adopt of its own accord when displaying its beauty, then, one directs the horse to appear joyous and magnificent, proud and remarkable for having been ridden.

Xenophon (430–355 B.C.E.)

806. A gentle horse with a soft bit will turn of its own wit.

Greene, *Carol.* (ca. 1500).

807. A horseman should know neither fear nor anger.

James Rarey

808. The horse will leap over trenches, will jump out of them, will do anything else, provided one grants him praise and respite after his accomplishment.

Xenophon (430–355 B.C.E.)

809. A horse is the matter and subject whereupon the art worketh, and is a creature sensible, and therefore so far as he is moved to do any thing, he is thereunto moved by sense and feeling.

Further, this is common to all sensible creatures, to shun all things as annoy them, and to like all such things as do delight them.

John Astley (d. 1595),
The Art of Riding . . . (1584).

810.   They say that princes learn no art truly, but the art of horsemanship. The reason is, the brave beast is no flatterer. He will throw a prince as soon as his groom.

Ben Jonson (1573–1637),
Explorata: Illiteratus Princeps (1636).

811.   Beauty, delicacy and position—these were the foundations of courtly equestrianism.

Henning Eichberg,
*Leistung, Spannung,
Geschwindigkeit* (1978).

812. I assert without fear of contradiction that gymnastics and horsemanship are as suitable to women as to men.

Plato (427–347 B.C.E.), *Laws*,
in Guttman, *Woman's Sports* (1991).

813. It [horseback riding] coarsened the voice and complexion, twisted the body, bestowed a masculine air and "produced an unnatural consolidation of the bones of the lower part of the body, enduring a frightful impediment of future function, which need not be dwelt on."

Kathleen E. McCrone (1941–) commenting on
Donald Walker's 1836 work, *Exercises for Ladies*,
in *Playing the Game: Sport and the Physical
Emancipation of English Women, 1870–1914* (1988).

814. The horse and his rider hath he thrown into the sea.

Exodus 15:1

815. In the black moon
of the highwaymen
the spurs sing.
          Little black horse.
Wither with your dead rider?

Frederico García Lorca (1898–1936),
Cancion de Jinete, 1860 (1921–1924).

816. If the horse does not enjoy his work, his rider will have no joy.

H.-H. Isenbart (1923–?),
in Isenbart and Bührer,
The Kingdom of the Horse (1969).

817. [The mind of man is as an] unbroken horse that would go anywhere except where you wanted it to.

St. Theresa of Avila (1515–1582)

818. No one can teach riding so well as a horse.

C.S. Lewis (1898–1963),
The Horse and His Boy (1954).

819. Throw your heart over the fence, and your horse will follow.

anon.

820. The rider casts his heart over the fence, the horse jumps in pursuit of it.

H.-H. Isenbart (1923–?),
in Isenbart and Bührer,
The Kingdom of the Horse (1969).

821. A Yorkshireman, like a dragoon, is nothing without his horse.

Robert Smith Surtees (1803–1864)

822. Dragoon. A soldier who combines dash and steadiness in so equal measure that he makes his advances on foot and his retreats on horseback.

Ambrose Bierce (1842–1914),
The Devil's Dictionary (1881–1906).

823. The rifle, effective as it is, cannot replace the effect produced by the speed of the horse, the magnetism of the charge, and the terror of cold steel.

Cavalry Training Manual, UK (1907),
in Blainey, The Causes of War (1973).

824. I've discovered a gap—a cavalry gap. The Russian Army has 3,000 horses and our Army has only 29 and never uses them except for military funerals. We should be on our guard. What if it turns out the Russians are coming by horse?

Eugene McCarthy (1916–), in
The New York Times, September 4, 1976.

825. If any of you is despondent because we are without horsemen and the enemy has many, let him remember that ten thousand horsemen are nothing but ten thousand men. Nobody ever lost his life in battle from the bite or kick of a horse. Besides, we are on far surer footing than horsemen. They hang on their horse's backs, afraid of falling off. Horsemen do have one advantage over us—retreat is safer for them than it is for us, and faster.

Xenophon (430–355 B.C.E.)

826. I have just read your dispatches about some sore-tongued and fatigued horses. Will you pardon me for asking what the horses of your army have done since the battle of Antietam that fatigues anything?

Abraham Lincoln (1809–1865), telegram
(October 24, 1862) to Gen. George McClellan (1826–1885),
in Nicolay and Hay, Complete Works of A. Lincoln, 8 (1905).

827. In one respect a cavalry charge is very like ordinary life. So long as you are all right, firmly in your saddle, your horse in hand, and well armed, lots of enemies will give you a wide berth. But as soon as you have lost a stirrup, have a rein cut, have dropped your weapon, are wounded, or your horse is wounded, then is the moment when from all quarters enemies rush upon you.

Winston Churchill (1874–1965), My Early Years (1930).

828. . . . so passionate a love of horses, and of hunting, that neither bodily infirmity, great age, nor mental incapacity, prevented his daily participation in the dangers of the chase.

Edgar Allan Poe (1809–1849), *Metzengerstein* (1931).

829. [Fate is] a little like a horse with a loose rein. It can meander calmly, or break into a gallop without warning, leaving you to hang on for dear life.

Howard Weinstein (1954?–), *Star Trek the Next Generation No. 19: Perchance to Dream* (1991).

830. Competitions are for horses, not artists.

Bela Bartok (1881–1945)

831. They ride in ranks of two,
a double nocturne in serge.
The sky, so they fancy, is a showcase of spurs.

Frederico García Lorca (1898–1936),
Romance de la Guardia Civil Española (1928).

832. An uncomplicated horse can be messed up with enough "schooling."

Cooky McClung, "Rules of the Day,"
The Chronicle of the Horse, October 7, 1983.

833. In order to make a horse, one must first create a rider.

Stephanie Lile, "The Renaissance: An Art Form Reborn,"
in Mellin, *The Morgan Horse* (1986), as reprinted
in *The USDF Bulletin* 15, no. 2 (1988).

834. Dressage is a living art . . . The creation of a partnership between two individuals—a horse and a rider—and that cannot be bought or sold.

Joanna Fowler, D.V.M., in
The USDF Bulletin 18, no. 1 (Spring 1991): 21.

835. In riding classical dressage, the goal is not to be the best, the goal is to be perfect.

Wendy Meyers, in *The USDF Bulletin* 18,
no. 1, (Spring 1991): 21.

836. Riding isn't just something you do to the horse, but something you and the horse do together.

Matthew Mackay-Smith,
in *Equus* 130 (August 1988).

837. You can ride any horse in a halter if he's broke.

Kiff Parrish, in *Practical Horseman* 17,
no. 2 (February 1989).

838. The horse and rider are inseparable. A horse would continue to be a horse if it had no rider, but without a horse a rider is nothing.

Stephanie Lile, "The Renaissance: An Art Form Reborn,"
in Jeanne Mellin, *The Morgan Horse* (1986;
as reprinted in *The USDF Bulletin* 15, no. 2 [1988]).

839. Riding: the art of keeping a horse between yourself and the ground.

The London Times

840. Moderation for all things; but if you have a passion for westerns, at least go ride a horse.

Patricia D. Cornwell, "Having Something to Say,"
in *The Writer* 104, no. 12 (December 1991).

841. Apparently, no one can tell people how to deal with horses better than horses themselves.

Emily Kilby, in *Equus* 130 (August 1988).

842. Wherever man has left his footprint in the long ascent from barbarism to civilization we will find the hoofprint of the horse beside it.

anon.

843. For the wonderful brain of man,
However mighty its force,
Had never achieved its lordly plan
Without the aid of the horse.

Ella Wheeler Wilcox (1850–1919)

844. He was an Anglo-Irishman.
In the blessed name of God, what's that?
A Protestant with a horse.

Brendan Behan (1923–1964), *The Hostage*, act 1 (1958).

845. My little horse must think it queer
To stop without a farmhouse near.

Robert Frost (1874–1963), *Stopping by the
Woods on a Snowy Evening*, st. 2 (1923).

846. He is glued to the high horse and won't
come down.

O. Henry (1862–1910), *Sphinx Apple* (1907).

847. My temper is just now for action ripe,
On the high horse my courage sits astride.

Moliere (1622–1673), *Sganarelle ou
Le Cocu imaginaire*, sc. 11 (1660).

848. He is on his high horse, spoken when people fall into a passion.

James Kelly, *Scottish Proverbs* (1721).

849. There are no handles to a horse, but the 1910 model has a string to each side of its face for turning its head when there is something you want it to see.

Stephen Leacock (1869–1944),
"Reflections on Riding," in *Literary Lapses* (1910).

850. Ride a free horse to death, and never mind what becomes of him afterwards.

Dykes, *English Proverbs* (1709).

851. According to the proverb, one may ride a free horse to death.

William Ellis (1798–1869),
The Modern Husbandman (1850).

852. Ride not a free horse to death.

Spanish proverb

853. A horse is his who mounts it.

French proverb

854. The world is exactly like a vicious horse,
which knows perfectly well when it is ridden
by one who cannot manage it properly; it
despises him, tries to get him out of the saddle,
and when it has succeeded in throwing him,
begins kicking him.

> Bruno (1548–1600), *Spaccio della Bestia*
> *Trionfanta*. Dialog 1, 1 (Sofia).

855. Behind the horseman sits black care.

> Horace (65–8 B.C.E.), *Odes*, bk. 3 (23 B.C.E.).

856. Care sits behind the horseman on the cantle
of his saddle. Ambition may also be detected
clinging somewhere about his spurs.

> G. J. Whyte-Melville (1821-1878),
> *Market Harbor* (1861).

857. The appearance of them is as the appearance
of horses; As horsemen so do they run.

> Joel 2:4

858. The horse thinks one thing, and he that rides
him another.

> John Ray (1627–1705), *English Proverbs* (1670).

859. The horse will go according as it is held by the bridle.

Indian (Kashmiri) proverb

860. A good feeling after the ride is better than winning a prize.

Bertalan de Nemethy, in Isenbart and
Bührer, *The Kingdom of the Horse* (1969).

861. And I looked, and behold, a pale horse: and his name that sat on him was Death.

Revelation 6:8

862. Until you can ride a horse, ride an ox.

Japanese proverb

863. The horse is the most willing when he is the most tormented.

Icelandic proverb

864. Care for your horse as though he were a friend, ride your horse as though he were an enemy.

Turkish proverb

865. You ride as you like on your own horse.

Russian proverb

866. To finish is to win.

motto of the American Endurance Ride Conference

867. Once a horse is born, someone will be found to ride it.

Hebrew proverb

868. When the horse comes to the edge of the cliff it is too late to draw the rein.

Chinese proverb

869. It is good riding in a safe harbour.

English proverb

870. Spare the lash, my boy, and hold the reins more firmly.

Ovid (43 B.C.E.–17 C.E.), *Metamorphoses*, bk. 2 (7 C.E.).

871. A horseman better than Bellerophon himself.

Horace (65–8 B.C.E.) referring to the
rider of Pegasus, *Odes*, bk. 3 (23 B.C.E.).

872. He will go mad on a horse who's proud on a pony.

Scottish proverb

873. A horse misus'd upon the road,
Calls to heaven for human blood.

William Blake (1757–1826),
Augries of Innocence (1803).

874. You will hear the beat of a horse's feet,
And the swish of a skirt in the dew,
Steadily cantering through
The misty solitudes,
As though they perfectly knew
The old lost road through the woods—
But there is no road through the woods!

Rudyard Kipling (1865–1936),
The Way Through the Woods.

875. Better ride on a pad, than on the horse
bare back.

John Heywood (1497–1580), *Proverbs* (1564).

876. ... Vaulted with such ease into his seat,
As if an angel dropp'd down from the clouds,
To turn and wind a firey Pegasus
And witch the world with noble horsemanship.

William Shakespeare (1564–1616),
Henry IV, pt. 1, act 4, sc. 1 (1597).

877. Give your horse a Welsh bait.

> Thomas Fuller (1608–1661), *History of the Worthies of England*, vol. 3 (1662) [to give your horse a rest on reaching the top of a hill].

878. Well could he ride, and often men would say,
"That horse his mettle from his rider takes:
Proud of subjection, noble by the sway,
What rounds, what bounds, what course,
what stop he makes!"
And controversy hence a question takes,
Whether the horse by him became his deed,
Or he his manage by the well-doing steed.

> William Shakespeare (1564–1616), *A Lover's Complaint* (1609).

879. When one is on horseback, he knows all things.

> George Herbert (1593–1633), *Jacula Prudentum* (1640)

880. Horseback, eh! . . . Ay, that's a prescription better than all your doctor's stuff.

> Francis Edward Smedley (1818–1864), *Frank Fairleigh*, ch. 41 (1850).

881. There's nothing like the first horseback ride to make a person feel better off.

> Herbert V. Prochnow (1897–?),
> *The Speaker's and Toastmaster's Handbook* (1990).

882. He who is on horseback will not spare his own father alive.

> Indian (Hindi) proverb

883. Be kind to the horse that carries you.

> Turki (Turkestan) proverb

884. Ride softly, that we may come sooner home.

> John Ray (1627–1705), *English Proverbs* (1678).

885. He grew into his seat;
And to such wondrous doing brought his horse,
As he had been incorpsed and demi-natured
with the brave beast.

> William Shakespeare (1564–1616),
> *Hamlet*, act 4, sc. 7 (1600).

886. A boisterous horse must have a rough bridle.

> Thomas Draxe (d. 1618) , *Bibliotheca Scholastica
> instructissima* (1616); also John Clarke (1609–1676),
> *Paroemiologia* (1639).

887. The seat on a horse makes gentlemen of some
and grooms of others.

> Miguel de Cervantes Saavedra (1547–1616),
> *Don Quixote de la Mancha* (1605–1616).

888. So that his horse, or charger, hunter, hack,
Knew that he had a rider on his back.

> George Gordon, Lord Byron (1788–1824),
> *Don Juan*, canto 14, st. 32 (1819–1824).

889. A rider unequaled—a sportsman complete,
A rum one to follow, a bad one to beat.

> G. J. Whyte-Melville (1821–1878), *Hunting Song*.

890. Lord Ronald said nothing; he flung himself
from the room, flung himself upon his horse and
rode madly off in all directions.

> Stephen Leacock (1869–1944), "Gertrude the Governess,"
> in *Nonsense Novels* (1917).

891. He who hires the horse should ride first.

> J. C. Bridge, *Cheshire Proverbs* (1917).

892. The use the Whip, the Horse complains,
Who have no Sense to use the Reins.

> Arthur Guiterman (1871–1943),
> *A Poet's Proverbs* (1924).

893. To hold the reins.

proverb [meaning to be in control]

894. Such horses are
The jewels of the horseman's hands and thighs,
They go by the word and hardly need the rein.

Stephen Vincent Benét (1898–1943),
John Brown's Body, bk. 4 (1928).

895. There has to be a woman, but not much of
one. A good horse is much more important.

Max Brand [Frederick Faust] (1892–1944)
on his philosophy of writing Westerns,
in *The New York Times*, September 16, 1985.

896. Treat a horse like a woman and a woman like
a horse, and they'll both win for you.

Elizabeth Arden (1878–1966),
in Lewis, *Miss Elizabeth Arden* (1972).

897. Keep one leg on one side,
the other leg on the other side,
and your mind in the middle.

Henry Taylor (1942?–), *Riding Lesson*.

898. One might compare the relation of the ego to the id with that between a rider and his horse. The horse provides the locomotor energy, and the rider has the prerogative of determining the goal and guiding the movements of his powerful mount towards it. But all too often in the relations between the ego and the id we find a picture of the less ideal situation in which the rider is obliged to guide his horse in the direction in which it itself wants to go.

> Sigmund Freud (1856–1939), "The Anatomy of the Mental Personality," lecture 31, *New Introductory Lectures on Psychoanalysis* (1932).

899. A horse's misbehavior will be in direct proportion to the number of people watching you ride him.

> Cooky McClung, "The Rules of the Day," in *The Chronicle of the Horse*, October 7, 1983.

900. In ancient times, to ride a horse was the surest sign of aristocracy (a warhorse, of course, and not a plow horse).

> Isaac Asimov (1920–1992), introduction to Asimov, Greenberg and Waugh, *Cosmic Knights*, Isaac Asimov's Magical Worlds of Fantasy, no. 3 (1984).

901. Most nations, free ones especially, should be dealt with like a spirited horse, whom a judicious rider will keep steady, by maintaining an exact balance in his seat, showing neither fear nor cruelty, occasionally giving and checking the rein, while he prudently and resolutely corrects with the spur, or kindly blandishes with his hand.

> Francis Gentleman (1728–1784),
> *A Trip to the Moon* (1764).

902. A made horse, and a man unarm'd are the fittest for use.

> Randle Cotgrave (d. 1634), entry at "cheval,"
> in *A Dictionarie of the French and English Tongues* (1611).

903. Necessity is as a strong rider with sharp stirrups, who maketh the sorry jade do that which the strong horse sometime will not do.

> James Justinian Morier (1780–1894),
> The *Adventures of Haji Baba of Ispahan* (1824)
> ["sharp spurs" would make more sense].

904. No rider wears sharper spurs than necessity.

> L. Sprague deCamp (1907–) and
> Catherine Crook deCamp (1907–),
> *The Incorporated Knight* (1973).

905. The high-spirited horse is controlled with the shadow of the whip, while the slug can hardly be made to move with the spurs.

Fra Bartolommeo Da San Concordio (1475–1517),
Giunta agli Ammaestramenti degli Antichi, 163.

906. The horse is here to stay, but the automobile is only a novelty—a fad.

President of the Michigan Savings Bank (1903)
advising Henry Ford's lawyer not to invest
in the Ford Motor Company.

907. When you set out to prove that a particular horse is a complete pig, he'll perform like a star . . . and vice versa.

Cooky McClung, "The Rules of the Day,"
The Chronicle of the Horse, October 7, 1983.

908. Steeds decked with purple and with tapestry,
With golden harness hanging from their necks,
Champing their yellow bits, all clothed in gold.

Virgil (70–19 B.C.E.), Aeneid, bk. 7 (19 B.C.E.).

909. One horse, one saddle.

William Scarborough,
Chinese Proverbs, no. 2704 (1875).

910.   Even a good horse cannot wear two saddles.

Chinese proverb

911.   One saddle is enough for one horse.

Thomas Fuller (1654–1734),
Gnomologia, no. 3791 (1732).

912.   He is a weak horse that is not able to bear
the saddle.

Scottish proverb

913.   A wounded horse trembles when he sees
the saddle.

Greek proverb

914.   Judging the horses by the saddles and
furniture, consider not oft times under a clownish
coat, is hidden a noble and lively understanding.

Stefano Guazzo (1530–1593),
Civil Conversations (1574).

915.   You may know the horse by his harness.

John Clarke (1606–1676), *Paroemiologia* (1639);
also John Ray (1627–1705), *English Proverbs* (1670)].

916. A horse is neither better nor worse for his trappings.

Thomas Fuller (1654–1734),
Gnomologia, no. 217 (1732).

917. You can't judge a horse by its harness.

Harold W. Thompson (1891–1964),
Body, Boots and Britches (1940).

918. The horse is not judged by the saddle.

German proverb; also a Chinese proverb

919. A thoroughbred horse is not dishonored by its saddle.

Syrian proverb

920. The fault of the horse is put on the saddle.

George Herbert (1593–1633),
Jacula Prudentum (1640).

921. A horse that will not carry a saddle, must have no oats.

Thomas Fuller (1654–1734),
Gnomologia, no. 218 (1732).

922. Lay the saddle on the right horse.

proverb

923. An old friend is like a ready saddled horse.

Afghani proverb

924. Wring not a horse on the withers, with a false saddle.

John Lyly (1554–1606),
Euphues and his England (1580).

925. It's all right to live on a horse—if it's your horse.

"Judge Roy Bean" [played by Walter Brennan
(1894–1974)] in *The Westerner* (1940); screenplay
by Joseph Swerling (1897–?) and Niven Busch (1903–?).

926. "Water polo? Isn't that dangerous?"
"I'll say! I had two ponies drown under me."

"Sugar" [played by Marilyn Monroe (1926–1962]
and "Joe" [played by Tony Curtis (1925–)]
in *Some Like It Hot* (1959); screenplay
by Billy Wilder (1906–?) and I. A. L. Diamond (1920–?).

927. There's one thing I do know—what this family needs is discipline. I've been a pretty patient man—but when people start riding horses up the front steps and parking them in the library, that's going a bit too far.

"Alexander Bullock" [played by Eugene Pallette
(1889–1954] in *My Man Godfrey* (1936);
screenplay by Morrie Ryskind (1895–1985).

928. In those days the horse was virtually a costar. The kids all knew that the Lone Ranger's mount was Silver and Roy Rogers rode Trigger. But who could tell you, years later, the name of Jim Arness' horse or Paladin's or what the Cartwrights called theirs? Not for nothing were they called horse operas.

Gene Autry (1907–), in Rothel,
The Great Show Business Animals (1980).

929. A horse is the greatest vehicle for action there is.

John Wayne (1907–1979),
in Hintz, *Horses in the Movies* (1979).

930. Itzig, where are you riding to?
Don't ask me, ask the horse.

Sigmund Freud (1856–1939),
letter (July 7, 1898) to Wilhelm Fliers,
in Freud, *Origins of Psychoanalysis* (1950).

931. He that strives not to stem his anger's tide,
Does a wild horse without a bridle ride.

Colley Cibber (1671–1757),
Love's Last Shift, act 3, sc. 7 (1696).

932. A man in passion rides a mad horse.

Benjamin Franklin (1706–1790),
Poor Richard's Almanack (1749).

933. If the horse is mad, he who sits upon it is
not also mad.

African (Ga) proverb

934. You never really learn how to swear until you
learn how to ride.

Cooky McClung, "Rules of the Day,"
The Chronicle of the Horse, October 7, 1983.

935. Jeffdavis rides a white horse,
Lincoln rides a mule;
Jeffdavis is a gentleman,
And Lincoln is a fool.

Southern doggerel (ca. 1863)

936. They say he rides as if he's part of the horse,
but they don't say which part.

Robert Sherwood (1896–1955),
commenting on Tom Mix

937. Buffalo Bill's
defunct
who used to
ride a watersmooth-silver stallion . . .

> e.e. cummings (1894–1962), "Portraits, Buffalo Bill's,"
> in *Complete Poems 1913–1962* (1972).

938. Never were abilities so much below
mediocrity so well rewarded; no, not [even]
when Caligula's horse was made consul.

> John Randolph of Roanoake (1772–1833)
> about Richard Rush (1780–1859) being
> appointed Treasury secretary (1826).

939. It's not right for a race horse to despise the
pace of a pony.

> African (Hausa) proverb

940. Ascot is so exclusive that it is the only
racecourse in the world where the horses own
the people.

> Art Buchwald (1925–), "Ordeal at Ascot,"
> *I Chose Caviar* (1957).

941. The pitiful little thing has to do with horse racing; and you might perhaps say that it is by Imbecility out of Staggering Incompetence.

Bernard Levin, review of the play *Dazzling Prospect* in *The Daily Express* (1961), in Rigg, *No Turn Unstoned* (1983).

942. One horse in the racecourse runs the fastest.

African (Hausa) proverb

943. A fine horse runs on by observing the shadow of the whip.

Japanese proverb

944. Many race horses are given peculiar names, especially if they don't finish among the first three.

anon.

945. Everyone knows that horse-racing is carried on mainly for the delight and profit of fools, ruffians and thieves.

George Gissing (1857–1903), *The Private Papers of Henry Ryecroft* (1903).

946. The spirited horse, which will of itself strive to win the race, will run still more swiftly if encouraged.

Ovid (43 B.C.E.–18 C.E.),
Epistoloe Ex Ponto, 2 (9 C.E.).

947. The valiant horse races best, at the barrier's fall, when he has others to follow and overpass.

Ovid (43 B.C.E.–18 C.E.),
Ars Amatoria, 3 (ca. 1 B.C.E.).

948. You can't take too much hold of a horse.

William Shoemaker (1931–), in
The New York Times, April 9, 1990.

949. Competition makes a horse-race.

Ovid (43 B.C.E.–18 C.E.)

950. We put all our money on the wrong horse.

Robert Arthur Talbot Gascoyne-Cecil,
Third Marquis of Salisbury (1830–1903),
speech (January 19, 1897).

951. A dark horse, which had never been thought of . . . rushed past the grandstand in sweeping triumph.

Benjamin Disraeli (1804–1881),
The Young Duke (1831).

952. A lean horse for a long race.

Montague, *Broadway Stomach* (1940).

953. The riders in a race do not stop short when they reach the goal. There is a little finishing canter before coming to a standstill. There is time to hear the voice of friends and to say to oneself "the work is done."

Oliver Wendell Holmes (1841–1935)
radio address (March 8, 1931).

954. There are, they say, fools, bloody fools, and men who remount in a steeplechase.

John Oaksey (1929–?), in *The Guardian* (1971).

955. Horse racing is an industry of hope. And in an industry of hope, there's always someone being taken for a ride.

William Tew, *Equus* 133 (November 1988).

956. Horse racing is animated roulette.

Roger Khan, "Intellectuals and Ball Players"
in *American Scholar*, November 3, 1957.

957. I bet my money on the bob-tail nag,
Somebody bet on de bay.

> Stephen Collins Foster (1826–1864),
> "Camptown Races" (1850).

958. The only man who makes money following the races is the one who does so with a broom and shovel.

> Elbert Hubbard (1856–1915),
> *The Roycroft Dictionary and Book of Epigrams* (1923).

959. Our culture doesn't include horse racing to the degree some others do. Queen Elizabeth owns a stable, but could you see President Nixon attending a yearling sale?

> Win Elliot in *The Washington Post*,
> February 11, 1970.

960. Horse sense is what a horse has that keeps him from betting on people.

> W.C. Fields (1880–1946)

961. In choosing the winner of a horse race, a good guess may beat all the skill and all the special knowledge in the world.

> Robert Lynd (1879–1949),
> *The Peal of Bells* (1925).

962. Lord Hippo suffered fearful loss
By putting money on a horse
Which he believed, if it were pressed,
Would run far faster than the rest.

> Hilaire Belloc (1870–1973),
> "Lord Hippo,"in *More Peers* (1911).

963. The chase, the sport of kings,
Image of war without its guilt.

> William Somerville (1675–1742)

964. Differences of opinion make horse races
and lawsuits.

> Erle Stanley Gardner (1889–1970),
> *The Case of the Drowsy Mosquito* (1943).

965. Any horse can be beaten on any given day.

> Angel Cordero, Jr. (1942–)

966. It can be set down in four words: the best of
everything. The best hay, oats and water.

> James "Sunny Jim" Fitzsimmons,
> commenting on what's needed to train
> a winning racehorse, in *Life*, June 18, 1963.

967. A long road tests a horse.

> Chinese proverb

968. One must plow with the horses one has.

German proverb

969. . . . Some people, who as soon as they have got upon a young horse . . . fancy that by beating and spurring they will make him a dress'd [trained] horse in one morning only. I would fain ask such stupid people, whether, by beating a boy, they could teach him to read, without first showing him his alphabet.

William Cavendish, Marquis of Newcastle (1592–1676),
New Method of Dressing Horses (1743).

970. Good horses make short miles.

George Herbert (1593–1633), Jacula Prudentum (1640).

971. Woe worth the chase, woe worth the day,
That cost thy life, my gallant grey.

Sir Walter Scott (1771–1832),
The Lady of the Lake, canto 1 (1810).

972. It takes a good deal of physical courage to ride a horse. This, however, I have. I get it at about forty cents a flask, and take it as required.

Stephen Leacock (1869–1944),
"Reflections on Riding," in Literary Lapses (1910).

973. From the American cowboy to the 12-year-old heroine of National Velvet, anyone who can master a horse seems master of his own fate. The ability to ride a horse—especially in the days before the automobile—has always been associated with freedom and independence.

Lynn Schnurnberger, *Let There Be Clothes* (1991).

974. All I say is, if you cannot ride two horses you have no right in the circus.

James Maxton (1885–1946), in
the *Daily Herald*, January 12, 1931.

975. They are scarce of horses where two ride on a dog.

English proverb

976. Dear to me is my bonny white steed;
Oft has he helped me at pinch of need.

Sir Walter Scott (1771–1832),
The Lay of the Last Minstrel, 4 (1805).

977. They'd like to see him riding a elephant, surrounded by horses; not trampled by elephants and kicked by horses.

Burmese proverb

978. Who drives the horses of the sun
shall lord it but a day.

John Vance Cheney (1848–1922),
The Happiest Heart (1905).

979. Night's son was driving
His golden-haired horses up;
Over the eastern firths
High flashed their manes.

Charles Kingsley (1819–1875),
The Longbeard's Saga.

980. The driving is like the driving of Jehu the
son of Nimshi; for he driveth furiously.

II Kings 9:20

981. Drive your horse with oats, not with a whip.

Yiddish proverb; also Russian proverb

982. It is not the horse but the oats that draw the cart.

Russian proverb

983. He loads not when he lists that wants both
horse and cart.

Randle Cotgrave (d. 1634), entry at "charger,"
in *A Dictionarie of the French and English Tongues* (1611).

984. He that hath neither Horse, nor Cart, cannot always load.

Wodroephe, *Spared Hours* (1623).

985. We know that the tail must wag the dog, for the horse is drawn by the cart;
    But the Devil whoops, as he whooped of old,
    It's clever, but is it Art?

Rudyard Kipling (1865–1936),
The Conundrum of the Workshops (1892).

986. A four-horse team cannot overtake the tongue.

Japanese proverb

987. A word which flew out of the mouth like a sparrow cannot be drawn back, even by four horses.

Czech proverb

988. The master's horse and one's own whip make fast driving.

Latvian proverb

989. Ill-matched horses draw badly.

Dutch provrb

990. As good horses draw in carts, as coaches.

Robert Burton (1577–1640),
Anatomy of Melancholy, pt. 2 (1621).

991. The wagon rests in winter, the sleigh in summer, the horse never.

Yiddish proverb

992. The best carriage horses are those which can most steadily hold back against the coach as it trundles down the hill.

Anthony Trollope (1815–1882),
Phineas Redux (1874).

993. Love and marriage, love and marriage,
Go together like a horse and carriage. . . .

Sammy Cahn (1913–?),
"Love and Marriage" (1955).

994. He'll never catch it, not with a chariot and
four white horses.

Titus Maccius Plautus (254–184 B.C.E.),
Asinaria (ca. 200 B.C.E.).

995. There is a touch of divinity even in brutes, and
a special halo about a horse, that should forever
exempt it from indignities. As for those majestic,
magisterial truck-horses of the docks, I would as
soon think of striking a judge on the bench, as
to lay violent hands upon their holy hides.

Herman Melville (1819–1891), *Redburn* (1849).

996. Like horses in a mill, drudging on in the same
eternal round.

Charles Lamb (1775–1834),
Last Essays of Elia: The Superannuated Man (1825).

997. The horse next the mill carries all the grist.

English proverb

998. The slow horse reaches the mill.

Irish proverb

999. The fat ox desires the trappings of the horse; the horse desires to plow.

Horace (65–8 B.C.E.), *Epistles*, bk. 1 (20 B.C.E.).

1000. Every horse thinks his own pack heaviest.

Thomas Fuller (1654–1734), *Gnomologia* (1732).

1001. All lay the load on the willing horse.

Thomas Draxe (d. 1618), *Bibliotheca Scholastica
instructissima* (1633); also Ray (1627–1705),
English Proverbs (1670), and
Fuller (1654–1734), *Gnomologia* (1732).

1002. The willing horse is always most ridden.

English proverb

1003. The horse which draws always get the whip.

French proverb

1004. He putteth the cart before the horse.

John Florio (1553–1625), *First Fruits* (1578).

1005. Set the cart before the horse.

John Heywood (1497–1580), *Proverbs* (1564).

1006. Having, as usual, set the cart before the horse, and taken the effect for the cause.

> Charles Kingsley (1819–1875),
> *The Water-Babies* (1863).

1007. I'll put my cart before the horse, like Homer.

> Cicero (106–43 B.C.E.), *Ad Atticum* (61 B.C.E.).

1008. That's putting the cart before the horse. . . .

> Samuel Z. Arkoff (1918–), commenting on
> his practice of coming up with movie
> titles and sales campaigns before the script
> is written, in Weaver, *Interviews with
> B Science Fiction and Horror Movie Makers* (1988).

1009. That techer setteth the carte before the horse that preferreth imitacyon before perceptes.

> Robert Whittington (fl. 1490–1548), *Vulgaria* (1520).

1010. May not an ass know when the cart draws the horse?

> William Shakespeare (1564–1616),
> *King Lear*, act 1, sc. 4 (1604).

1011. Evil comes by cart-loads, and goes away by ounces, comes on horse-back, and goes away afoot.

English proverb

1012. Only a man harrowing clods
In a slow silent walk
With an old horse that stumbles and nods
Half asleep as they stalk.

Thomas Hardy (1840–1928), "In Time of
the Breaking of Nations," in Moments of Vision (1917).

1013. Why does
a hearse horse
snicker
　Hauling a
lawyer away?

Carl Sandburg (1878–1967),
"The Lawyers Know
Too Much," in
Smoke and Steel (1920).

1014. To make the plough go before the horse.

James I of England [James VI of Scotland]
(1566–1625), letter (July 1617) to the Lord Keeper.

1015. If you do not see a harnessed horse don't yearn for a trip.

Mexican-American proverb

1016. I will not change my horse with any that treads on four pasterns. Ça, ha! he bounds from the earth, as if his entrails were hairs, le cheval volant, the Pegasus, chez les narines de feu! When I bestride him, I soar, I am a hawk: he trots the air; the earth sings when he touches it; the basest horn of his hoof is more musical than the pipe of Hermes . . . he is pure air and fire . . . the prince of palfreys; his neigh is like the bidding of a monarch and his countenance enforces homage.

William Shakespeare (1564–1616),
Henry V, act 3, sc. 7 (1598).

1017. The bounding steed you pompously bestride, shares with his lord the pleasure and the pride.

Alexander Pope (1688–1744),
An Essay on Man, 3 (1733).

1018. Go anywhere in England where there are natural, wholesome, contented and really nice

English people; and what do you always find?
That the stables are the real center of the
household.

George Bernard Shaw (1856–1950),
Heartbreak House, act 3 (1913).

1019. Wilt thou lend me thy mare to ride but a mile?
No, she's lame, going over a stile;
But if thou wilt her to me spare,
Thou shalt have money for thy mare.
Ho, ho, say you so!
Money shall make my mare to go.

unknown, *The Second Part of Musicks Melodie* (1609).

1020. In . . . need a man that has no horse will go
on foot. . . .

J.R.R. Tolkien (1892–1973),
The Lord of the Rings, pt. 2,
The Two Towers, rev. ed. (1965).

1021. My friend, judge me not,
Thou seeist I judge not thee.
Betwixt the stirrup and the ground
Mercy I asked, and mercy I found.

William Camden (1551–1623),
Remains Concerning Britain (1605).
[epitaph of a man killed by a fall from his horse]

1022. When you're young and you fall off a horse, you may break something. When you're my age and fall off, you splatter.

Roy Rogers (1911–),
in Colombo, *Popcorn in Paradise* (1979).

1023. A horse; make sure you get one that complements your height. If you're 4'8" and want to look "tall in the saddle," consider getting a pony. Also pick a horse you're sure won't throw you. Getting thrown off your horse in front of a girl makes you look dumb.

Lynn Schnurnberger,
Let There Be Clothes (1991).

1024. There is no secret so close as that between a rider and his horse.

Robert Smith Surtees (1803–1864),
Mr. Sponge's Sporting Tour, ch. 31 (1853).

1025. A horse knows its rider.

African (Hausa) proverb

1026. You look for the horse you ride on.

Russian proverb

1027. There are only two classes in good society in England: the equestrian classes and the neurotic classes.

George Bernard Shaw (1856–1950), *Heartbreak House* (1913).

1028. The hallmark of a true equestrian is a passionate interest in all things pertaining to horses.

Sharon Ralls Lemon, in Edwards, *The Ultimate Horse Book* (1991).

1029. Strictly speaking, I cannot swear that being kicked in the stomach by a horse would be an experience preferable to seeing this play by Signor Giuseppe Marotti . . . because I have never been kicked in the stomach by a horse.

But I have seen this play, and I can certainly say that if a kick in the stomach by a horse would be worse, I do not wish to be kicked in the stomach by a horse.

And I can certainly add that, unpleasant though the prospect of being kicked in the stomach by a horse may be, I would certainly rather be kicked in the stomach by a horse than see the play again.

Bernard Levin review of *Out of This World*,
in *The Daily Express* (1960),
in Rigg, *No Turn Unstoned* (1983).

1030. Four things greater than all things are,
Women and Horses and Power and War.

Rudyard Kipling (1865–1936), *Ballad of the King's Jest.*

1031. Three jolly gentlemen,
In coats of red,
Rode their horses,
Up to bed.

Walter de la Mare (1873–1956), *The Huntsmen.*

1032. Ride a cock-horse to Banbury Cross,
To see a fine lady upon a white horse,
Rings on her fingers and bells on her toes,
And she shall have music wherever she goes.

nursery rhyme

1033. I sprang to the stirrup, and Joris, and he;
I galloped, Dirk galloped, we galloped all
three.

Robert Browning (1812–1889),
How they Brought the Good News From Ghent to Aix.

1034. My foot in the stirrup, my pony won't stand,
Goodbye, Old Paint, I'm a-leavin' Cheyenne.

anon. cowboy song, "Goodbye Old Paint"

1035. Foot in the stirrup and hand on the horn,
Best damned cowboy ever was born.

anon. cowboy song, "The Old Chisholm Trail"

1036. Up hill spare me,
Down hill forbear me;
Plain way, spare me not,
Nor let me drink when I am hot.

Thomas Fuller (1654–1734), *Gnomologia* (1732).

1037. I pray that gentle hands
May guide my feet;
I ask for kind commands
From voices sweet;
At night a stable warm
With scented hay,
Where, safe from every harm,
I'll sleep till day.

unknown (British), "Pony's Prayer"

1038. Hack: a horse to be ridden with one hand
while its owner flirts with a lady companion.

E. Hartley Edwards (1927–),
The Ultimate Horse Book (1991).

1039. An unwilling horse is more trouble than walking.

"Augustus" [played by Brian Blessed (1937–)] in "Family Affairs" episode (1976) of the television series *I, Claudius*; screenplay by Jack Pulman (1928–1979).

1040. To ride on the horse with ten toes.

proverb [meaning to walk on your own feet]

1041. To ride on shank's mare [is to walk on your own shanks, or legs].

proverb

1042. Dear Priscus, don't ride on that hard-pulling mare,
Or gallop so fast in pursuit of the hare.
Too often the hunter turns victim, and lies
Where he fell off his horse, never more to arise.
Though you still skirt the hedge and the ditch and the wall,

The plain's hidden perils may give you a fall.
You'll see lots of riders come off, every Meet.
Let's hope they are lucky and land on their feet!
If you must have blood-sports, take a tip from
a friend,
The more dangerous game brings less risk in
the end.
Let's go and hunt boar; with your galloping habits
You'll come to more grief than you bring to
the rabbits.

Martial [Marcus Valerius Martialis]
(ca. 40–103), in Anderson,
Horses and Riding (1980).

1043. Start we swiftly with steeds unsaddled—
Hence to battle with brandished swords!

old Norse poem

Part Four
Unicorns and Others

1044. Now I will believe that there are unicorns.

William Shakespeare (1564–1616),
The Tempest, act 3, sc. 3 (1611).

1045. The lion and the unicorn
Were fighting for the crown;
The lion beat the unicorn
All around the town.
Some gave them white bread,
And some gave them brown;
Some gave them plum cake,
And sent them out of town.

nursery rhyme

1046. God himself must needs be traduced, if
there is no unicorn.

Edward Topsell (1658)

1047. One by one in the moonlight there,
Neighing far off on the haunted air,
The unicorns come down to the sea.

Conrad Aiken (1889–1973), "Evening Song" (1914).

1048. Although unicorns have little reason to believe
in us, the least we can do is believe in them.

Paul Johnsgard (1931–) and Karin Johnsgard (1964–),
Dragons and Unicorns a Natural History (1982).

1049. Redeem

the time. Redeem
the unread vision in the higher dream
While jeweled unicorns draw by the gilded hearse.

T.S. Eliot (1888–1965),
Ash-Wednesday, ch. 4 (1930).

1050. There are in India certain wild asses which are as large as horses, and larger. Their bodies are white, their heads dark red, and their eyes dark blue. They have a horn on the forehead which is about a foot and a half in length. . . . The base of this horn, for some two hands'-breath above the brow, is pure white; the upper part is sharp and of a vivid crimson; and the remainder, or middle portion, is black. . . . Other asses, both the tame and the wild, and in fact all animals with solid hoofs, are without the ankle bone and have no gall in their liver, but these have both the ankle-bone and the gall. This ankle-bone . . . is as heavy as lead and its colour is that of cinnabar through and through. The animal is exceedingly swift and powerful, so that no creature, neither the horse nor any other, can overtake it.

Ctesias (415 B.C.E.)

1051. The Unicorn—noble, chaste, fierce yet
  beneficent,
        altruistic though solitary, strangely beautiful . . .

Odell Shepherd,
The Lore of the Unicorn (1956).

1052. The unconquerable nature of God is likened
  to that of a unicorn.

St. Basil (330–379),
commentary on Psalm 28.

1053. The unicorn is noble,
  He knows his gentle birth,
  He knows that God has chosen him
  Above all beasts of earth.

Ludwig Uhland (1787–1862),
Alte hoch-und-niederdeutche Volkslieder, no. 337 (1844).

1054. And the lovliest of all was the unicorn.

The Irish Rovers, "The Unicorn" (1971).

1055. What are the four Intelligent Creatures?
    The Unicorn, the Phoenix, the Tortoise,
  and the Dragon.

traditional Chinese saying

1056. If indeed there is a heaven, one can only hope that its gates are wide enough to accommodate the largest of all dragons and its horizons sufficiently remote to allow the shyest unicorn to graze in peace forever.

Paul Johnsgard (1931–) and Karin Johnsgard (1964–),
Dragons and Unicorns a Natural History (1982).

1057. In a world suffering from pollution, the unicorn can purify water with a single dip of its horn. In a world where animals are becoming extinct, the unicorn can never die . . . The unicorn symbolizes sensitivity coupled with strength, the lure of sexuality and nature linked with the power of purity and truth.

Nancy Hathaway (1946–), *The Unicorn* (1980).

1058. Will the unicorn be willing to serve thee, or abide by thy crib?

Job 39:9

1059. Unicorns can thrive anywhere the heart and imagination are receptive to them.

Paul Johnsgard (1931–) and Karin Johnsgard (1964–),
Dragons and Unicorns a Natural History (1982).

1060. Like as a Lyon, whose imperiall powre
A prowd rebellious Unicorn defyes,
T'avoide the rash assault and wrathfull stowre
Of his fiers foe, him to a tree applies,
And when him running in full course he spies,
He slips aside; the whiles that furious beast
His precious horne, sought of his enimies,
Strikes in the strocke, ne thence can be releast,
But to the mighty victor yields a bounteous feast.

Edmund Spenser (1552–1599),
The Fairie Queen, bk. 2, canto 5, sec. 10 (1589).

1061. The ultimate visual image of the unicorn: a
graceful, horse-like animal, creamy white, with a
long spiraling horn, cloven hoofs, a curled beard,
and a delicately plumed tail.

Nancy Hathaway (1946–) , The Unicorn (1980)
[this is the unicorn depicted in the Unicorn Tapestries
hanging in The Cloisters, New York] .

1062. I saw there two and thirty unicorns. They
are a cursed sort of creature much resembling a
fine horse, unless it be that their heads are like a

stag's, their feet like an elephant's, their tails like a white boar's, and out of each of their foreheads sprouts a sharp black horn.

François Rabelais (1494–1553),
Pantagruel (1532).

1063. On the Canadian border [of Maine], there are sometimes seen animals resembling horses, but with cloven hoofs, rough manes, a long straight horn upon the forehead, a curled tail like that of the wild boar, black eyes, and a neck like that of a stag. They live in the loneliest wilderness.

Dr. Olfert Dapper (seventeenth century)

1064. Jill had . . . quite fallen in love with the unicorn. She thought—and she wasn't far wrong—that he was the shiningest, delicatest, most graceful animal she had ever met, and he was so gentle and soft of speech that, if you hadn't known, you would hardly have believed how fierce and terrible he could be in battle.

C.S. Lewis (1898–1963),
The Last Battle (1956).

1065. And the first animal he named was the unicorn. And when the Lord heard the name Adam had spoken, He reached down and touched the tip of the single horn growing from the animal's forehead. From that moment on, the unicorn was elevated above other beasts.

Nancy Hathaway (1946–),
The Unicorn (1980).

1066. A truly wise man never plays leapfrog with a unicorn.

"Banacek" [played by George Peppard (1928–)]
in the television series *Banacek* (1972–1973),
in Mingo and Javna, *Primetime Proverbs* (1989).

1067. For of all the animals the lion is the most majestic, and the unicorn the purest.

Nancy Hathaway (1946–),
The Unicorn (1980).

1068. That horse had wings for to flee.

Geoffrey Chaucer (1340–1400),
"The Squire's Tale" (ca. 1386),
The Canterbury Tales (1387).

1069. Oh! For a horse with wings.

William Shakespeare (1564–1616),
Cymbeline, act 3, sc. 2 (1609).

1070. Mesaphus, a son of Neptune god of the sea, who as poets faire, begat upon Medusa the winged horse, named Pegasus. . . .

Thomas Blundeville (fl. 1561),
*A Newe Book Containing the Arte of Ryding
and Breaking Greate Horses* (1560).

1071. Then whoso will with virtuous wing essay
To mount to heaven, on Pegasus must ride,
And with sweet Poet's verse be glorified.

Edmund Spenser (1552–1599),
The Fairie Queen (1589).

1072. . . . with his winged heels did tread the wind,
As he had been a foal of Pegasus his kind.

Edmund Spenser (1552–1599),
The Fairie Queen, bk. 1, canto 9, sec. 21 (1589).

1073. To break Pegasus' neck.

expression [meaning to write bad poetry]

1074. They swayed about upon a rocking horse,
And thought it Pegasus.

John Keats (1795–1821),
"Sleep and Poetry," in *Poems* (1817).

1075. [A] good rocking-horse has often more of the true horse about it than an instantaneous photograph of a derby winner.

Desmond McCarthy (1878–1952)

1076. . . . with large rocking-horse nostrils and teeth that you just know bite an apple every day.

Cecil Beaton, commenting on Katherine Hepburn (1907–), in Shipman, *Movie Talk* (1988).

1077. You'll ride on a horse that was foal'd of an acorn.

John Ray (1627–1705), commenting on a hobby-horse, *English Proverbs* (1670).

1078. Who hath noon hors on a staff may ride.

John Lydgate (1370–1451), *Political Poems* (1444).

1079. Centaur. One of a race of persons who lived before the division of labor had been carried to such a pitch of differentiation, and who followed the primitive economic maxim, "every man his own horse." The best of the lot was Chiron, who to the wisdom and virtues of the horse

added the fleetness of man. The scripture
story of the head of John the Baptist on a
charger shows that pagan myths have
somewhat sophisticated sacred history.

Ambrose Bierce (1842–1914),
The Devil's Dictionary (1881–1906).

1080. Centaurs were the result of mankind's
degeneration in the days of Enosh.

B'reishith Rabbah 23

1081. Some things, of course,
you can't change. Pretending
that you have is like painting
stripes on a horse and
hollering "zebra!"

Eddie Cantor (1892–1964), The Way I See It (1959).

1082. That white horse you see in the park could be
a zebra synchronized with the railings.

Ann Jellicoe (1927–?), The Knack, act 3 (1962).

1083. . . . [who appeared in] the likenesses of a
horse, carrying books.

Mohammed

1084. I should like to be a horse.

attributed to Queen Elizabeth II (1926–)

1085. If he must learn to ride a horse for a movie, he will watch that horse like no one else has watched a horse and when he does the scene he will be both horse and rider.

Stella Adler (1895–?),
commenting on Marlon Brando (1924–),
in Shipman, *Movie Talk* (1988).

1086. If I tell thee a lie, spit in my face, call me horse.

William Shakespeare (1564–1616),
Henry IV, pt. 1, act 2, sc. 4 (1597).

1087. Methinks I have a great desire to a bottle of hay; good hay, sweet hay, hath no fellow.

William Shakespeare (1564–1616),
A Midsummer Night's Dream, act 4, sc. 1 (1594).

1088. A giraffe is a horse designed by a committee.

anon.

1089. A camel is a horse designed by a committee.

anon.

1090. He who rides horse of wind with legs of wax melts in the sun.

Maltese proverb

1091. All music is folk music, I ain't never heard no horse sing a song.

Louis Armstrong (1901–1971),
in *The New York Times*, July 7, 1971.

1092. I'd horsewhip you if I had a horse.

Groucho Marx (1895–1977)

1093. A shoemaker makes shoes without leather,
Of all the elements taken together,
Earth, water, fire and air,
And every customer had two pair:
A horseshoe.

old rhyming riddle

1094. A horseshoe that clatters needs a nail.

Spanish proverb

1095. Happy thou art, as if every day thou hadst picked up a horseshoe.

Henry Wadsworth Longfellow (1819–1892),
Evangeline, pt. 1 (1847).

1096. In pitching horseshoes, the first rule is to remove the horse.

anon.

1097. I never play horseshoes, 'cause Mother taught us not to throw our clothes around.

"Mister Ed," the talking horse,
in the television show *Mister Ed* (1961–1966),
in Mingo and Javna, *Primetime Proverbs* (1989).

1098. I really am a horse doctor. But marry me and I'll never look at any other horse!

"Hugo Z. Hackenbush" [played by
Groucho Marx (1895–1977)] in
A Day at the Races (1937); screenplay
by Robert Pirosh (1910–1989),
George Seaton (1911–1979), and
George Oppenheimer (1900–1977).

1099. When I appear in public, people expect me to neigh, grind my teeth, paw the ground and swish my tail—none of which is easy.

Princess Anne (1950–), in
The Observer, May 22, 1977.

1100. SIXTY HORSES WEDGED IN A CHIMNEY. The story to fit this sensational headline has not yet turned up.

J. B. Morton (1893–1979), "Mr. Justice Cocklecarrot: Home Life," in *The Best of Beachcomber*.

1101. A carousel horse off the machine is nothing more than a wooden statue.

Gail Hall, in Hinds, *Grab the Brass Ring* (1990).

1102. Hippogriff. An animal (now extinct) which was half horse and half griffin. The griffin itself was a compound creature, half lion and half eagle. The hippogriff was actually, therefore, only one-quarter eagle, which is two dollars and fifty cents. The study of zoology is full of surprises.

Ambrose Bierce (1842–1914), *The Devil's Dictionary* (1881–1906).

1103. Men, my dear, are very queer animals, a mixture of horse-nervousness, ass-stubbornness, and camel-malice, with an angel bobbing about unexpectedly like the apple in the posset, and when they can do exactly as they please, they are very hard to drive.

Thomas Huxley (1825–1895), letter (February 10, 1895) to Mrs. W. K. Clifford.

1104. Why is it that a woman will forgive homicidal behavior in a horse yet be highly critical of a man for leaving the toilet seat up?

> Dave Barry (1947–), "Wit's End: Horsefeathers," in *The Washington Post Magazine*, July 28, 1991.

1105. A mare's nest.

> proverb [meaning something that doesn't exist]

1106. And as for mare's nests, I've never had the faintest notion what they were . . . I suppose they're in the category of hen's teeth . . . and snake's hips?

> D. Ogburn, *Will* (1935).

1107. And with great lies about his wooden horse
Set the crew laughing, and forgot his course.

James Elroy Flecker (1884–1915), Old Ships (1915).

1108. Sing of the building of the horse of wood, which Epeius made with Athene's help, the horse which once Odysseus led up into the citadel as a thing of guile, when he had filled it with the men who sacked Ilios.

Homer (fl. 850 B.C.E.), The Odyssey, bk. 8 (ca. 850 B.C.E.).

1109. Trust not the horse, ye Trojans.

Virgil (70–19 B.C.E.),
The Aeneid, bk. 2 (19 B.C.E.).

Key Word Index

by quotation number, not page number

necks 102, 281, 908
neigh 42, 1016, 1099
neighing 1047
neighs 97, 432
nose 15, 27, 37, 177
noses 133
nostril 283
nostrils 141, 177, 1076

oats 151, 202, 212, 215, 226,
    227, 230–232, 272, 469, 562,
    921, 966, 981, 982
old 41, 82, 87, 89, 92, 95, 190,
    338, 548, 608, 874, 923, 973,
    985, 1034
oral cavity 27
outride 710
ox 186, 234, 259, 644, 862, 999
oxen 275

paint 1034
palfreys 1016
passion 73, 195, 840, 848, 932
passionate 828, 1028
pasterns 102, 1016
pasture 441
pastures 109
Pegasus 876, 1016, 1070–1074
people 18, 103, 202, 435, 498,
    502, 503, 544, 701, 841, 848,
    899, 927, 940, 960, 969, 1018,
    1099
person 75, 697, 881
persons 71, 1079
piebald 30, 31
plough 1014
plow 900, 968, 999
plows 234
polo 926
ponies 926

pony 503–505, 746, 775, 872,
    939, 1023, 1034
poverty 152, 153
prances 107, 446

race 546, 944, 946, 952, 953,
    961, 1079
racecourse 940, 942
races 446, 947, 958, 964
rein 141, 827, 829, 868, 894, 901
reins 546, 870, 892, 893
remount 954
ridden 748, 805, 854, 1002, 1038
ride 16, 89, 299, 341, 573, 583,
    624, 626, 696, 698, 706, 708,
    709, 711, 722, 740, 746, 748,
    754, 755, 756, 770, 774, 793,
    795, 831, 837, 840, 850–852,
    860, 862, 864, 865, 867, 875,
    878, 881, 884, 891, 899, 900,
    931, 934, 937, 955, 972–975,
    1019, 1026, 1032, 1040–1042,
    1071, 1077, 1078, 1085
rider 283, 458, 670–672, 675,
    764, 765, 767, 772, 773, 802,
    814–816, 820, 833, 834, 838,
    878, 888, 889, 898, 901, 903,
    904, 1024, 1025, 1085
riders 447, 953, 1042
rides 7, 537, 575, 627, 651, 673,
    675, 758, 768, 769, 858, 932,
    935, 936, 1090
riding 31, 697, 791, 793, 794,
    803, 818, 835, 836, 839, 869,
    927, 930, 977
road 78, 143, 189, 721, 873,
    874, 967
roan 44, 59, 804
rode 721, 746, 890, 928, 1031
rodeoing 699

tires 330, 433, 761, *778, 779*
tooth 182, 183
trooper 686
trot 74, 110, 261, 779, 787
trots 427, 1016
trotting 766
turn 90, 180, 802, 806, 876
turned 105
turning 849
turns 544, 824, 1042

unarmed 687, 902
unbacked 133
unicorn 1045, 1046, 1051–1058,
    1060, 1061, 1064–1067
unicorns 1044, 1047–1049,
    1059, 1062
unsaddled 1043

walk 452, 477, 1012
walking 704, 1039
war 260, 963, 1030
warhorse 900
water 75, 366–368, 370–373,
    375–380, 423, 469, 535, 564,
    926, 937, 966, 1057, 1093

whinny 166–168
whip 318, 335, 362, 676, 681–
    683, 892, 905, 943, 981, 988,
    1003
whipped 746
whipping 332
whisked 120
white 32, 58, 109, 741, 775,
    976, 1045, 1050, 1061, 1062
whiteness 280
widow 190, 258, 530
wife 181, 189, 192, 385, 455,
    491, 492, 764
wild 109, 141, 392, 453, 557,
    594, 801, 1050, 1063
wing 1071
winged 1070, 1072
wings 402, 687, 1068, 1069
withers 173, 924
wives 115
woman 3, 261, 318, 493, 652,
    700, 895, 896, 1104
women 191, 438, 449, 450, 812,
    1030

zebra 1081, 1082

Author Index

by quotation number, not page number

Bibliography

Magazines and Newspapers

Arabian Horse World
Chronicle of the Horse
Equus
Practical Horseman
USDF Bulletin (Unites States Dressage Federation)
The Washington Post
The Washington Star
The Writer

Books

Adams, A. K. *Home Book of Humorous Quotations*. New York: Dodd, Mead, 1969.

Adams, Franklin Pierce. *FPA Book of Quotations*. New York: Funk & Wagnalls, 1952.

Anderson, J. K. *Horses and Riding*. Santa Barbara, CA: Bellerphon Books, 1980.

Andrews, Robert, ed. *The Concise Columbia Dictionary of Quotations*. New York: Columbia University Press, 1989.

Anthony, Piers. *Virtual Mode*. Book One, Mode Series. New York: Ace, 1991.

Asimov, Isaac, and Jason A. Shulman. *Isaac Asimov's Book of Science and Nature Quotations*. New York: Weidenfeld & Nicolson, 1988.

Asimov, Isaac, Martin H. Greenberg, and Charles G. Waugh, eds. *Cosmic Knights*. Isaac Asimov's Magical Worlds of Fantasy, no. 3. New York: Signet, 1984.

Apperson, George Latimer. *English Proverbs and Proverbial Phrases*. Detroit: Gale Research, 1969.

Auden, W. H., and Louis Kronenberger. *The Viking Book of Aphorisms*. New York: Penguin, 1981.

Augarde, Tony. *The Oxford Book of Modern Quotations*. Oxford, England: Oxford University Press, 1991.

Baker, Daniel B. *Political Quotations*. Detroit: Gale Research, 1990.

Baron, Joseph L. *A Treasury of Jewish Quotations*. New York: Crown, 1956.

Barry, Dave. *Dave Barry Talks Back*. New York: Crown, 1991.

Bartlett, John. *Bartlett's Familiar Quotations*. 15th & 125th Anniversary Editions. Boston: Little, Brown, 1980.

Baz, Petros D. *A Dictionary of Proverbs*. New York: Philosophical Library, 1963.

Bierce, Ambrose. *The Collected Writings of Ambrose Bierce*. Secaucus, NJ: Citadel, 1946.

Bingham, Colin. *Men and Affairs*. New York: Funk & Wagnalls, 1967.

Bohle, Bruce. *Home Book of American Quotations*. New York: Dodd, Mead, 1967.

Boyce, Charles. *Shakespeare A to Z*. New York: Facts on File, 1990.

Bradley, John P., et al. *The International Dictionary of Thought*. Chicago: J. G. Ferguson, 1969.

Bradley, Marion Zimmer. *Thendara House*. New York: DAW, 1983.

Braude, Jacob M. *Speaker's and Toastmaster's Handbook of Anecdotes By and About Famous Personalities*. Englewood Cliffs, NJ: Prentice Hall, 1971.

———. *Speaker's Encyclopedia of Stories, Quotations, and Anecdotes*. Englewood Cliffs, NJ: Prentice Hall, 1955.

———. *Lifetime Speaker's Encyclopedia*, vols. 1 and 2. Englewood Cliffs, NJ: Prentice Hall, 1962.

Brotchie, Susan W. *Old Horseman's Almanak 1976*. Beverly, MA: TRT Publications, 1975.

Brown, Raymond Lamont. *A Book of Proverbs*. Newton Abbot, Devon, England: David & Charles, 1970.

Browning, D. C. *Everyman's Dictionary of Quotations and Proverbs*. London: J. M. Dent, 1951.

Browning, D. C. *Everyman's Dictionary of Shakespeare Quotations*. London: J. M. Dent, 1961.

Brussell, Eugene C. *Dictionary of Quotable Definitions*. Englewood Cliffs, NJ: Prentice Hall, 1970.

Bullfinch, Thomas. *The Age of Fable*. New York: Heritage Press, 1958.

Byrne, Robert. *The 637 Best Things Anybody Ever Said*. New York: Atheneum, 1982.

Cambridge Biographical Dictionary. Cambridge, England: Cambridge University Press, 1990.

Carruth, Gorton, and Eugene Erlich. *The Harper Book of American Quotations*. New York: Harper, 1988.

Cerf, Christopher, and Victor Navasky. *The Experts Speak*. New York: Pantheon, 1984.

Champion, Selwyn Gurney. *Racial Proverbs*. London: Routledge & Kegan Paul, 1950.

Chapin, John, ed. *The Book of Catholic Quotations*. New York: Ferrar, Strauss, 1956.

Charlton, James. *The Writer's Quotation Book*. New York: Pushcart Press, 1985.

Cheviot, Andrew. *Proverbs, Proverbial Expressions, and Popular Rhymes of Scotland*. Paisley, Scotland: Alexander Gardner, 1896.

Cohen, J. M., and M. J. Cohen. *The Penguin Dictionary of Modern Quotations*. 2d ed. Harmondsworth, Middlesex, England: Penguin, 1980.

———. *The Penguin Dictionary of Quotations*. New York: Viking, 1977.

Cole, William. *Poems One Line and Longer*. New York: Grossman, 1973.

Colombo, John Robert. *Popcorn in Paradise: The Wit and Wisdom of Hollywood*. New York: Holt, Rinehart & Winston, 1979.

Conlin, Joseph R. *Morrow Book of Quotations in American History*. New York: Morrow, 1984.

Conn, George H. *The Arabian Horse in Fact, Fantasy and Fiction*. New York: Arco, 1959.

Contemporary Authors. Various editions. Detroit: Gale Research.

Cooke, H. L. *Dogs, Horses, Cats and Other Animals in the National Gallery of Art*. Richmond, VA: Westover, 1970.

Copeland, Lewis, and Faye Copeland. *10,000 Jokes, Toasts and Stories*. New York: Doubleday, 1965.

Copper, Marcia S. *The Horseman's Etiquette Book*. New York: Charles Scribner's Sons, 1976.

Crisp, Quentin. *Quentin Crisp's Book of Quotations*. New York: Macmillan, 1989.

Current Biography and *Current Biography Yearbook*. Various editions. New York: H. W. Wilson.

Current Biography Cumulated Index 1940-1985. New York: H. W. Wilson, 1986.

Davidoff, Henry. *A World Treasury of Proverbs*. New York: Random House, 1946.

Dantith, John, and Amanda Isaacs. *Medical Quotes: A Thematic Dictionary*. New York: Facts on File, 1989.

DeCamp, L. Sprague, and Catherine Crook deCamp. *The Incorporated Knight*. New York: Baen, 1987.

DeLoach, Charles. *The Quotable Shakespeare*. Jefferson, NC: McFarland, 1988.

Delano, Isaac O. *Yoruba Proverbs*. Ibadan, Nigeria: Oxford University Press, 1966.

Dossenbach, Monique, and Hans D. Dossenbach. *The Noble Horse*. New York: Portland House, 1987.

Edelhart, Mike, and James Tinen. *America the Quotable*. New York: Facts on File, 1983.

Edwards, Elwyn Hartley. *The Ultimate Horse Book*. New York: Dorling Kindersley, 1991.

Edwards, Tryon. *The New Dictionary of Thoughts*. New York: Standard Book Co., 1961.

Eisel, Deborah Davis, and Jill Swanson Reddig. *Dictionary of Contemporary Quotations*, vol. 5. N.p.: John Gordon Burke, 1981.

Encyclopedia Britannica. Chicago: Encyclopedia Britannica, Inc., 1970.

Esar, Evan. *20,000 Quips and Quotes*. New York: Doubleday, 1968.

Evans, Bergen. *Dictionary of Quotations*. New York: Delacorte, 1968.

Evans, Ivor H. *Brewer's Dictionary of Phrase and Fable*. 14th ed. New York: Harper & Row, 1989.

Fabricant, Noah D. *Amusing Quotations for Doctors and Patients*. New York: Grune & Stratton, 1950.

Farber, Bernard E. *A Teacher's Treasury of Quotations*. Jefferson, NC: McFarland, 1985.

Ferguson, Rosalind. *Facts on File Dictionary of Proverbs*. New York: Facts on File, 1983.

Field, Claud. *A Dictionary of Oriental Quotations (Arabic and Persian)*. New York: Macmillan, 1911.

Flesch, Rudolph. *The New Book of Unusual Quotations*. New York: Harper & Row, 1966.

Foreman, Max L. *The World's Greatest Quotations*. New York: Exposition Press, 1970.

Gaffney, Sean, and Cashman, Seamuc. *Proverbs and Sayings of Ireland*. Dublin: Wolfhound Press, 1974.

Gassner, John, and Edward Quinn, eds. *The Reader's Encyclopedia of World Drama*. New York: Crowell, 1969.

Gayley, Charles Mills. *Classic Myths*. Lexington, MA: Xerox, 1939.

Glazer, Mark. *A Dictionary of Mexican American Proverbs*. New York: Greenwood, 1987.

Green, Jonathon. *Morrow's International Dictionary of Contemporary Quotations*. New York: Morrow, 1982.

Griffith, Joe. *Speaker's Library of Business Stories, Anecdotes, and Humor*. Englewood Cliffs, NJ: Prentice Hall, 1990.

Gross, John. *Oxford Book of Aphorisms*. Oxford, England: Oxford University Press, 1983.

Guttman, Allen. *Women's Sports: A History*. New York: Columbia University Press, 1991.

Hale, Judson, ed. *The Best of The Old Farmer's Almanac: The First 200 Years*. New York: Random House, 1991.

Halliwell, Leslie. *Halliwell's Filmgoer's Companion*. 9th ed. New York: Charles Scribner's Sons, 1988.

Harbottle, Thomas Benfield. *Dictionary of Quotations — Classical*. New York: Frederick Ungar, 1958.

Harbottle, Thomas Benfield, and Philip Hugh Dalbiac. *Dictionary of Quotations — French and Italian*. New York: Frederick Ungar, 1958.

Hart, Henry H. *Seven Hundred Chinese Proverbs*. Stanford, CA: Stanford University Press, 1937.

Hathaway, Nancy. *The Unicorn*. New York: Viking, 1980.

Haun, Harry. *The Movie Quote Book*. New York: Lippincott & Crowell, 1980.

Hausdorff, David M. *A Book of Jewish Curiosities*. New York: Crown, 1955.

Henry, Lewis C. *Five Thousand Quotations for All Occasions*. New York: Doubleday, 1945.

Hinds, Anne Dion. *Grab the Brass Ring: The American Carousel*. New York: Crown, 1990.

Hintz, H. F. *Horses in the Movies*. South Brunswick, NJ: Barnes, 1979.

Hla Pe, U. *Burmese Proverbs*. London: John Murray, 1962.

Houghton, Patricia. *A World of Proverbs*. Poole, Dorset, England: Blandford, 1981.

Howey, M. Oldfield. *The Horse in Magic and Myth*. New York: Castle, 1958.

Hyman, Robin. *The Quotation Dictionary*. New York: Macmillan, 1962.

Ions, Veronica. *Egyptian Mythology*. Vol. of *The Library of the World's Myths and Legends*. New York: Peter Bedrick, 1982.

Isenbart, H.-H., and E. M. Bührer. *The Kingdom of the Horse*. Lucerne, Switzerland: C. J. Bucher, 1969.

Jackman, Michael. *Crown's Book of Political Quotations*. New York: Crown, 1982.

———. *The Macmillan Book of Business and Economic Quotations*. New York: Macmillan, 1984.

Jobes, Gertrude. *Dictionary of Mythology Folklore & Symbols*. New York: Scarecrow, 1962.

Johnsgard, Paul, and Karin Johnsgard. *Dragons and Unicorns A Natural History*. New York: St. Martin, 1982.

Jones, Hugh Percy. *Dictionary of Foreign Phrases and Classical Quotations*. Edinburgh, Scotland: John Grant, 1963.

Katz, Ephraim. *The Film Encyclopedia*. New York: Harper & Row, 1979.

Kenin, Richard, and Justin Wintle. *The Dictionary of Biographical Quotation*. New York: Knopf, 1978.

Kenrick, Vivienne. *Horses in Japan*. London: J. A. Allen, 1964.

Kin, David, ed. *Dictionary of American Maxims*. New York: Philosophical Library, 1959.

King, Anita. *Quotations in Black*. Westport, CT: Greenwood, 1981.

Knudson, R. R., and Mary Swenson. *American Sports Poems*. New York: Orchard Books, 1988.

Kumove, Shirley. *Words Like Arrows*. New York: Shocken, 1985.

Kunitz, Stanley J. *Twentieth Century Authors*. First Supplement. New York: H. W. Wilson, 1955.

Kunitz, Stanley J., and Vineta Colby. *European Authors 1000-1900*. New York: H. W. Wilson, 1967.

Kunitz, Stanley J., and Howard Haycroft. *American Authors 1600- 1900*. New York: H. W. Wilson, 1938.

———. *British Authors Before 1800*. New York: H. W. Wilson, 1952.

———. *British Authors of the Nineteenth Century*. New York: H. W. Wilson, 1936.

———. *Twentieth Century Authors*. New York: H. W. Wilson, 1942.

Lederer, Richard. *Anguished English*. New York: Dell/Laurel, 1989.

———. *Crazy English*. New York: Pocket Books, 1989.

LeShan, Lawrence. *How to Meditate*. New York: Bantam, 1974.

Lewis, Alec. *The Quotable Quotations Book*. New York: Crowell, 1980.

Lewis, C. S. *The Horse and His Boy*. The Chronicles of Narnia. New York: Collier, 1954.

————. *The Last Battle*. The Chronicles of Narnia. New York: Collier, 1954.

Lieberman, Gerald F. *3,500 Good Quotes for Speakers*. New York: Doubleday, 1983.

Little, Charles E. *Historical Lights 1885*. New York: Funk & Wagnalls, 1885.

Lindsey, John, M.D.. *Medical Quotations From English Prose*. Boston: Richard G. Badger, 1924.

Lofficier, Jean-Marc. *Doctor Who: The Programme Guide*. rev. ed. London: Target, 1989.

Lunde, Paul, and Justin Wintle. *A Dictionary of Arabic and Islamic Proverbs*. London: Routledge & Kegean Paul, 1984.

Mackey, Alan L. *The Harvest of a Quiet Eye*. Bristol, England: The Institute of Physics, 1977.

Macmillan Dictionary of Quotations. New York: Macmillan, 1989.

Magill, Frank N. *Magill's Quotations in Context*. New York: Harper & Row, 1965.

————. *Magill's Quotations in Context*. 2d series. New York: Harper & Row, 1969.

————, ed. *Critical Survey of Poetry*. English Language Series. Englewood Cliffs, NJ: Salem Press, 1982.

McGraw Hill Encyclopedia of World Biography. New York: McGraw-Hill, 1973.

McKenna, Michael. *The Stein and Day Dictionary of Definitive Quotations*. New York: Stein & Day, 1983.

McMahon, Sean. *A Book of Irish Quotations*. Springfield, IL: Templegate, 1946.

McMurray, Emily, and Wiloch, Thomas. *Contemporary Authors Cumulative Index*. Detroit: Gale Research, 1991.

Mead, Frank S. *The Encyclopedia of Religious Quotations*. Westwood, NJ: Fleming H. Revell, 1965.

Menken, H. L. *A New Dictionary of Quotations*. New York: Knopf, 1942.

Mercatante, Anthony J. *Zoo of the Gods*. New York: Harper & Row, 1974.

Metcalf, Fred. *Penguin Dictionary of Modern Humorous Quotations*. New York: Viking Penguin, 1986.

Mieder, Wolfgang. *Prentice Hall Encyclopedia of World Proverbs*. Englewood Cliffs, NJ: Prentice Hall, 1986.

Mingo, Jack, and John Javna. *Primetime Proverbs: The Book of TV Quotes*. New York: Harmony, 1989.

Murphy, Edward F. *2,715 One-Line Quotations for Speakers, Writers and Raconteurs*. New York: Crown, 1981.

Murphy, Edward F. *The Crown Treasury of Relevant Quotations*. New York: Crown, 1978.

Nash, Jay Robert, and Stanley Ralph Ross. *The Motion Picture Guide*. vol. 5. Chicago: Cinebooks, 1986.

New Larousse Encyclopedia of Mythology. London: Hamlyn, 1959.

Nicolson, J. U. *Canterbury Tales in Modern English*. Garden City, NY: Garden City Books, 1934.

Nyembezi, C. L. *Zulu Proverbs*. Johannesburg, South Africa: Witwatersrand University Press, 1963.

Oxford Dictionary of Quotations. 3d ed. Oxford, England: Oxford University Press, 1979.

Partnow, Elaine. *The Quotable Woman 1800-1981*. New York: Facts on File, 1982.

———. *The Quotable Woman From Eve to 1799*. New York: Facts on File, 1985.

Pater, Alan F., and Jason R. Pater. *What They Said in 1969*. Beverly Hills, CA: Monitor, 1970. (also volumes for 1970-1978; 1982; 1985-1990).

Pearson, Heskith. *Common Misquotations*. London: Hamish Hamilton, 1973.

Pepper, Margaret. *The Harper Religious and Inspirational Quotation Companion*. New York: Harper & Row, 1989.

Peter, Laurence J. *Peter's Quotations: Ideas for Our Time*. New York: Morrow, 1977.

Platt, Suzy, ed. *Respectfully Quoted*. Washington, D.C.: Library of Congress, 1986.

Poe, Edgar Allan. *Complete Stories and Poems of Edgar Allan Poe*. New York: Doubleday, 1966.

Pound, Ezra, and Noel Stock, eds. *Love Poems of Ancient Egypt*. New York: New Directions, 1978.

Powell, David. *The Wisdom of the Novel*. New York: Garland, 1985.

Prochnow, Herbert V. *1,497 Jokes, Stories & Anecdotes*. New York: Sterling, 1982.

————. *Speaker's and Toastmaster's Handbook*. Rocklin, CA: Prima Publishing, 1990.

Prochnow, Herbert V., and Herbert V. Prochnow Jr. *A Treasure Chest of Quotations for All Occasions*. New York: Harper & Row, 1983.

————. *The Public Speaker's Treasure Chest*. 4th ed. New York: Harper & Row, 1986.

————. *The Toastmaster's Treasure Chest*. New York: Harper & Row, 1979.

Radice, Betty. *Who's Who in the Ancient World*. Harmondsworth, Middlesex, England: Penguin, 1973.

Reilly, John M., ed. *Twentieth Century Crime and Mystery Writers*. New York: St. Martins, 1980.

Rigg, Diana. *No Turn Unstoned*. New York: Doubleday, 1983.

Ringo, Miriam. *Nobody Said it Better!* Chicago: Rand McNally, 1980.

Robert, Kate Louise, ed. *Hoyt's New Cyclopedia of Practical Quotations*. New York: Funk & Wagnalls, 1940.

Rogers, James. *The Dictionary of Clichés*. New York: Facts on File, 1985.

Rosenberg, M. R. *Quotations for the New Age*. Secaucus, NJ: Citadel, 1978.

Rosten, Leo. *Leo Rosten's Treasury of Jewish Quotations*. New York: Bantam, 1972.

Rothel, David. *The Great Show Business Animals*. San Diego: Barnes, 1980.

Safire, William, and Safir, Leonard. *Good Advice*. New York: Times Books, 1982.

Schurnberger, Lynn. *Let There Be Clothes*. New York: Workman, 1991.

Seldes, George. *The Great Quotations*. Secaucus, NJ: Castle Books, 1966.

Shafritz, Jay M. *Words on War*. New York: Prentice Hall, 1990.

Shakespeare, William. *Hamlet*. New York: Signet Classics, 1963.

———. *A Midsummer Night's Dream*. New York: Washington Square Press, 1958.

———. *Richard II*. New York: Signet Classics, 1963.

———. *The Tempest*. New York: Signet Classics, 1963.

Shapiro, Nat. *Whatever It Is I'm Against It*. New York: Simon and Schuster, 1984.

Shepherd, Odell. *The Lore of the Unicorn*. New York: Harper, 1956.

Shipps, Anthony W. *The Quote Sleuth: A Manual for the Tracer of Lost Quotations*. Urbana, IL: University of Illinois Press, 1990.

Simpson, Anthony, and Sally Simpson. *The Oxford Book of Ages*. Oxford, England: Oxford University Press, 1985.

Simpson, J. A. *The Concise Oxford Dictionary of Proverbs*. Oxford, England: Oxford University Press, 1982.

Simpson, James B. *Simpson's Contemporary Quotations*. Boston: Houghton Mifflin, 1988.

Slaton, Lana. *Horses in History Coloring Album*. Los Angeles: Troubadour Press, 1987.

Smith, William George. *The Oxford Dictionary of English Proverbs*. 3d ed. Oxford, England: Oxford University Press, 1970.

Spenser, Edmund. *The Faerie Queene*. New York: Heritage Press, 1952.

Spevek, Marvin. *The Harvard Concordance to Shakespeare*. Cambridge, MA: Belknap Press of Harvard University Press, 1973.

Stapleton, Michael. *The Illustrated Dictionary of Greek and Roman Mythology*. New York: Peter Bedrick, 1978.

Steiner, Stan. *Dark and Dashing Horsemen*. San Francisco: Harper & Row, 1981.

Stevenson, Burton. *The Home Book of Proverbs, Maxims, and Famous Phrases*. New York: Macmillan, 1948.

———. *The Home Book of Quotations*. New York: Dodd, Mead, 1967.

———. *The Macmillan Book of Proverbs, Maxims and Famous Phrases*. New York: Macmillan, 1968.

———. *A Dictionary of Political Quotations*. London: Europa, 1984.

Strauss, Maurice B., ed. *Familiar Medical Quotations*. Boston: Little, Brown, 1968.

Strong, James. *Strong's Exhaustive Concordance of the Bible*. New York: Abingdon-Cokesbury, 1890.

Swift, Jonathan. *Gulliver's Travels*. New York: Heritage Press, 1940.

Taylor, Archer, and Bartlett Jere Whiting. *A Dictionary of American Proverbs and Proverbial Phrases 1820-1880*. Cambridge, MA: Belknap Press of Harvard University Press, 1958.

Tilley, Morris Palmer. *A Dictionary of the Proverbs in England in the Sixteenth and Seventeenth Centuries*. Ann Arbor: University of Michigan Press, 1950.

Tolkien, J.R.R. *The Lord of the Rings*. New York: Ballantine, 1965.

Tripp, Rhoda Thomas. *The International Thesaurus of Quotations*. New York: Prentice Hall, 1970.

Uris, Dorothy. *Say It Again*. New York: Dutton, 1979.

Valentine, Joseph W. *A Book of Cliches*. New York: Vanguard, 1963.

Van Buren, Maud. *Quotations for Special Occasions*. New York: H. W. Wilson, 1939.

Van Ekeren, Glenn. *The Speaker's Sourcebook*. Englewood Cliffs, NJ: Prentice Hall, 1988.

Vinson, James, ed. *Actors and Actresses*. The International Dictionary of Films and Filmmakers, vol. 3. Chicago: St. James, 1984.

Walsh, William S. *International Encyclopedia of Prose and Poetical Quotations*. Philadelphia: John C. Winston, 1951.

Watson, John T. *Dictionary of Poetical Quotations*. Philadelphia: Lindsey & Blakiston, 1847.

Weaver, Tom. *Interviews with B Science Fiction and Horror Movie Makers*. Jefferson, NC: McFarland, 1988.

Webster's Ninth New Collegiate Dictionary. Springfield, MA: Merriam Webster, 1991.

Webster's New Biographical Dictionary. Springfield, MA: Merriam Webster, 1983.

Weinstein, Howard. "Perchance to Dream." "Star Trek the Next Generation", no. 19. New York: Pocket Books, 1991.

White, T. H. *Mistress Masham's Repose*. New York: Putnam, 1946.

Whiting, Bartlett Jere. *Modern Proverbs and Proverbial Sayings*. Cambridge, MA: Harvard University Press, 1989.

———. *Proverbs, Sentences and Proverbial Phrases From English Writings Mainly Before 1500*. Cambridge, MA: Belknap Press of Harvard University Press, 1968.

Wilson, Don. *Treasury of Black Quotations*. Washington, D.C.: Interfair Press, 1987.

Wilson, F. P. *The Oxford Dictionary of English Proverbs*. 3d ed. Oxford, England: Oxford University Press, 1970.

Wilstach, Frank J. *A Dictionary of Similes*. Boston: Little, Brown, 1917.

Woods, Ralph. *The World Treasury of Religious Quotations*. New York: Hawthorne, 1966.

About the Author

Deborah Eve Rubin has ridden, owned, and worked around horses for more than thirty years. Although she took undergraduate courses in animal science and horse management, she returned to the University of Maryland later to earn a master's degree in Library Science. She has worked as an editorial indexer/researcher, an information specialist, a library technician, and a corporate librarian.

She now devotes most of her time to writing—and riding her two horses, which she finds time for almost every day. Her hobbies include photography, philately, miniatures, crafts, needlework, collecting anything related to horses, and reading.

Deborah is a member of the American Philately Society, The American Topical Society, and the American Horse Shows Association. She lives in Bethesda, Maryland.